D0562562

Disclaimer: The opinions presented herein are solely those of the author except where specifically noted. Nothing in the book should be construed as investment advice or guidance, as it is not intended as investment advice or guidance, nor is it offered as such. Nothing in the book should be construed as a recommendation to buy or sell any financial or physical asset. It is solely the opinion of the writer, who is not an investment professional. The publisher/author disclaims any implied warranty or applicability of the contents for any particular purpose. The publisher/author shall not be liable for any commercial or incidental damages of any kind or nature.

First edition published November 2016

Oftwominds.com
P.O. Box 4727
Berkeley, California 94704

Cover: Theresa Barzyk
Concept: G.F.B.

Inequality and the Collapse of Privilege

Of Two Minds Essentials [sm]

Charles Hugh Smith

Table of Contents

Introduction

No matter where we live, we're hearing more and more about *inequality* and *privilege*. Inequality appears to be rising globally, and we sense that rising inequality is inherently destabilizing, both politically and socially. It thus seems self-evident that if we are to achieve a stable society with widespread prosperity, we must identify the source of this rising inequality and do whatever is necessary to reverse it.

The first question we must ask is: why is the gulf between the wealthy and everyone else widening so dramatically? There is no one simple answer, and the causal factors are intertwined: monetary policies, globalization, technology and so on. But rather than immediately enter this thicket of complexity, let's start with the basic framework of any economy.

Broadly speaking, an economy extracts energy and natural resources and applies labor and capital to these resources to generate a surplus of goods and services that are distributed to the populace. This system can be organized to benefit the few at the expense of the many, or it can distribute the surplus more evenly.

Every economy operates within a social and political system. The social and political rules define how the economy works and how its surpluses are distributed.

In hierarchical societies dominated by elites, these social and political rules boil down to one dynamic: *privilege*. And privilege generates inequality, which eventually destabilizes the status quo.

What is Privilege?

So just what *is* privilege? There are many types of privilege, but they all share the following characteristic: *privilege delivers benefits, wealth and power that are unearned*.

Structurally, privilege is a *specific arrangement of power, opportunity, responsibility and risk (PORR; pronounced 'poor')*: the privileged transfer the responsibility for outcomes and the risks of loss to the unprivileged while maintaining a grip on opportunity, power and wealth.

In a privileged society and economic system, the primary function of the status quo (i.e. the people in control) is to protect the privileged and enforce this specific arrangement of power, opportunity, responsibility and risk that maintains their unearned wealth and power.

- Politically speaking, privilege is functionally equivalent to *autocracy*: the system's wealth and power are held by the privileged, while the responsibility and risk are pushed onto the powerless.
- Economically speaking, privilege is functionally equivalent to *monopoly*: the owners of a monopoly set the price above what a competitive market would charge and skim the unearned profit as *rentier fees*.

Stripped to its essence, privilege is nothing more than institutionalized racketeering.

Overview of Privilege and Destabilization

Any autocracy (which includes monopolies, oligarchies, state cartels, etc.) is inherently unstable, because privilege generates the following political double-bind:

- If the privileged keep a tight grip on wealth and power, the dispossessed eventually rise up.
- And if the system allows enough social mobility to create a middle class, that aspirational class will demand their fair share of the power.

So regardless of whether the system suppresses or enables social mobility, the end result is the same: the status quo is destabilized.

Privilege is destabilizing for other reasons as well. The dead weight of privilege reduces productivity, generates perverse incentives, and fuels social injustice. Innovation and competition are rightly viewed as threats to privileged monopolies - and are therefore suppressed.

The Importance of Eliminating Privilege

It is no accident that privileged monopolies are stagnant economically and socially, for they are incapable of producing the two foundations of widely distributed prosperity: *sustainable stability and productivity*.

There is a moral imperative to the eradication of privilege as well: privilege is immoral, as *rising inequality is the only possible output of privilege*. Privilege is exploitive, parasitic, predatory and destructive to the society and economy, and generates inequality by its very nature.

The only way to foster sustainable stability and productivity and reverse rising inequality is to systemically remove its source: privilege. And the only way to eliminate privilege is to change the system from the ground up by restructuring the *distribution of power, responsibility and risk*.

The privileged would have us believe that their hold on the top of the wealth/power pyramid is the natural order of human life, and they are quick to heap examples from history on anyone who questions their dominance: the few at the top of the pyramid have always ruled the many below.

But this self-serving view of human history is simply no longer true, because technological advancements are enabling *new non-hierarchical arrangements of power, responsibility and risk that are more stable and more productive than privileged hierarchical pyramids*.

The Internet is enabling networked collaboration and trade that is decentralized (peer-to-peer) and self-organizing: participants do not need a hierarchical chain of command to manage work flows, production or sales; the network adjusts without being centrally managed.

Compare the cost structure of a top-heavy hierarchy of multiple layers of managers and self-organizing networks: the network is far cheaper and more efficient. As technology improves, the productivity gap between hierarchies and networks widen: networks are more nimble and adapt to changing conditions faster than any hierarchy, and therefore they are inherently far more productive.

As these advancements widen the productivity/cost gap between privileged pyramids and more productive decentralized, networks, they will hasten the destabilization of high-cost, low-productivity privileged hierarchies, which will increasingly be unable to provide for both the privileged few and the unprivileged many.

Privilege will implode one way or another. The collapse can be messy and destructive, or it can be dynamic and fruitful.

A system that eliminates privilege works equally well for everyone because everyone has (to use Nassim Taleb's phrase) "*skin in the game*" (exposure to risk) and *equal access to opportunity*.

Eradicating privilege will not automatically solve problems such as resource depletion, but it will provide the foundation for equitable, flexible solutions that benefit the common good rather than the privileged few.

Only societies with shared purpose, social cohesion and flexible economies that offer opportunities for everyone will survive the disruptions ahead. These qualities are precisely what privilege destroys.

Privilege functions in complex and often subtle ways, and our first task to examine the structures that create and protect privilege.

Chapter One - Understanding Privilege

To more fully understand privilege, we can consider its traditional source: *birthright*, where an individual obtains unearned wealth and power by being born into a privileged family or class. But defining privilege by its source doesn't really describe the nature of privilege.

There are many manifestations of privilege, but they all share certain core characteristics. I have already noted the most important two:

1) the benefits of privilege are unearned; and
2) privilege is a specific distribution of power, opportunity, responsibility, risk—the PORR attributes: the privileged have the power to transfer accountability (i.e. responsibility for outcomes) and risk onto others, while skimming risk-free gains.

Privilege is ultimately the power to harvest the gains from positive outcomes while avoiding the losses that result from negative outcomes.

Let's add a third core characteristic:

3) *the privileged have opportunities that are not available to the unprivileged*.

Equality of Opportunities, Not Outcomes

Equality of outcomes is often confused with *equality of opportunity*. Some think equality means everyone should earn identical rewards for performing the same processes. But people's skills, aptitudes, and experience are inherently unequal, and so the outcomes of two people with the same education spending the same number of hours at a task will also be unequal.

When we speak of equality, that is, the eradication of privilege, we mean *equality of opportunity* and *equal exposure to the potential for gain and loss, i.e. risk*. Outcomes not only cannot be equalized, they shouldn't be equalized, for society as a whole gains when people are free to pursue their individual *comparative advantages*.

For example, if I love doing carpentry and I spend my spare time studying and pondering labor-saving tricks of the trade, the output (outcome) of my work will likely be much greater (quantitatively and/or qualitatively) than the output of someone who is uninterested in carpentry and is just going through the motions to earn a paycheck.

In a productive, non-hierarchical system stripped of privilege, people have the same opportunities to find work they find fulfilling or rewarding. If everyone is given the opportunity to maximize their output, each individual and society gain productivity and well-being. But outcomes will always be unequal, even in a system with equal opportunities for all. By eliminating privilege, we guarantee equality of opportunity, not outcomes.

What can be equalized is opportunity, responsibility and risk. If privilege is stripped out, everyone has equal opportunities for positive outcomes. There is no guarantee of positive outcomes, however, nor should there be, for exposure to risk is the necessary foundation for making productive choices.

Types of Privilege

Privilege is as complex as the economic, political and social orders that generate it. To understand how it is created and enforced, we must tease apart the intertwined dynamics of privilege in the financial, political and social orders.

Financial and political privileges manifest in formal institutions such as government and finance. In contrast, social privileges are a tangled snarl of informal systems, internalized biases, and primal emotions. So we'll start with the stickier complexities of social privilege; financial privilege is discussed in Chapter Four, while political privilege is addressed in Chapter Five.

Social Privilege

Humans have a finely-tuned sense of fairness, because fairness is a key dynamic in social groups. Privilege is inherently unfair, so we recognize it immediately.

But there are other sources of unfairness as well, *luck* being the most visible.

To understand privilege in a systemic fashion, we need to separate it from other sources of unfairness. Let's start by focusing on two key characteristics of privilege:

1) the benefits of privilege are unearned; and

2) privilege is a specific distribution of power, opportunity, responsibility and risk.

Essentially, the privileged have (unearned) opportunities to benefit from a rigged game that are unavailable to the unprivileged, and the privileged can push accountability and risk onto the unprivileged while securing the system's gains.

Risk plays a key role in privilege. The un(der)privileged must accept responsibility for outcomes as well as the risk that outcomes could be poor: choices are made, work is performed, and consequences follow. Those with privilege get benefits without having to accept (as much) responsibility or risk; their benefits flow not from being accountable and taking risks, but instead from the game being rigged in their favor.

In effect, *privilege has no skin in the game.*

It's easy to confuse benefits that are earned with benefits that are unearned (i.e. privilege). A recent article highlights the confusion. In an article entitled *Did You Do These 6 Activities Today? Then You've Got Class Privilege*, author Carmen Rios identified six activities as evidence of what she termed "class privilege":

1) getting a full night's sleep;

2) having enough cash to choose convenience;

3) being able to call in sick and be paid;

4) driving your car to work (or taking reliable public transit);

5) getting paid for all the hours you worked, and

6) being able to afford to buy fresh, healthy food.

But in reality, rather than privilege, these are *manifestations of income*: if someone has an upper-middle class job, these advantages are the direct result of the pay and benefits they are earning.

Clearly, life is easier for those earning high wages and benefits. But this is not the same as privilege, which bestows unearned advantages in a rigged game. What the essay is actually discussing is the difference between *disadvantaged* and *advantaged*, and the pathways leading from the *disadvantaged class* to the *advantaged class*.

The Pathway from the Disadvantaged Class to the Advantaged Class

Consider all the factors and decisions that go into the different outcomes of two equally disadvantaged people: one is still struggling to make ends meet while the other has climbed the ladder to a high income.

1) First, there's luck. Luck can be a major influence on how well we do in life. Some attractive people are discovered in the supermarket and go on to become Hollywood stars; others have a childhood friend who starts a company and offers them a job, etc.

2) Second, there are the decisions to pursue the conventional paths to middle-class financial security: earning an in-demand college degree with a predictable market value such as accounting, finance, math, management, etc. This path is easier for those with family wealth, but as immigrants continue to demonstrate, sacrifice and perseverance enable lower-income households to produce college graduates.

   There are also non-college pathways to high income, including acquiring skills in high-paying trades such as welding, pipefitting, etc., and starting trade-based service businesses.

3) Third, high income and financial security are correlated to a specific set of values that have been identified by surveys of self-made wealthy people. The authors of the book *The Millionaire Next Door: The Surprising Secrets of America's Wealthy* found that wealth accumulation requires not just sacrifice, discipline and hard work, but the independence required to be self-employed (two-thirds of self-made millionaires are self-employed, compared to less than 10% of the entire work force.)

   These wealthy households typically don't make much more than median incomes, but they save 20% or more of their income, habitually living below their means.

   In other words, becoming financially secure is less a matter of being in the top 5% of household income and more a matter of saving and investing a significant share of middle class incomes.

4) Fourth, there are social and familial factors that aid or inhibit financial security. Households with two wage-earners (typically a married or cohabitating couple) generally earn more than one-wage earner households. This one factor largely predicts the financial security of a household.

5) Fifth, there are innate genetic differences in ability between individuals. *Examples*: Even after extensive training, very few of us can memorize 45 minutes of highly complex classical music and play it with nuance and artistic expression. Studies have found the top scorers in the math section of the SAT test are far more likely to earn

a doctoral degree than the average student, and far more likely to obtain a patent than the average high-SAT score student. These people have extraordinary abilities, and so the outcomes of their efforts tend to be significantly greater than the rest of the field.

Note that all of these advantages are quite different from privilege.

Examples of Real Privilege   Trump

Let me give you an example of real privilege: being able to borrow $10 million at 0.75% interest without posting collateral worth $10 million. This $10 million can then be invested in low-risk Treasury bonds paying 2.75% (2% net annual interest), netting the privileged borrower $200,000 annually for doing zero work.

Here's another example: someone whose grandfather and father are alumni and generous donors to an Ivy League university. This student will receive preferential admission to the university. Bush - Yale

It's easy to confuse privilege with outcomes based on a variety of factors; our innate sense of fairness tells us it's unfair that some people have better luck, make better decisions, have more family support and more productive value systems.

So to be clear: privilege is not to be confused with differences in outcome due to luck, decisions or values: *privilege is the result of systems that are rigged in favor of the few at the expense of the many*.

This discussion allows us to see that eliminating privilege is not enough to level the playing field; society must also provide pathways to higher earnings and greater financial security for the disadvantaged.

In distinguishing between "privilege" vs. "unequal outcomes for the unprivileged", we can now describe the attributes of *privileged classes* that are largely inaccessible and *advantaged classes* that are accessible to everyone.

Privileged Classes vs. Advantaged Classes

Our analysis of privilege recognizes three basic classes: *disadvantaged, advantaged, and privileged*. Membership in a truly *privileged class* is inaccessible to the unprivileged, regardless of how hard they work or how many credentials they earn. Conversely, the *advantaged class* is accessible to everyone who qualifies based on ability, values and training.

What Carmen Rios describes is the *advantaged class* of high earners that is open to anyone with the requisite drive, ability to make long-term plans, make daily sacrifices for important goals, etc. As noted above, you don't need a PhD to become financially secure; operating a pest control business or welding shop is an equally open path to those who live below their means and invest the savings prudently.

While members of a privileged class may feel that they have earned their advantages, an apples-to-apples comparison with the unprivileged finds that the privileged class receives a premium above and beyond what the unprivileged receive when they do the same work and hold the same credentials.

It is a statistical fact that men in the managerial class generally earn significantly more than women doing the same work in the same career positions. Economists and sociologists attempt to explain this as being something other than mere social bias—for example, that women earn less because they devote more years to childcare, so men pile up more experience and leapfrog them in management—but the explanations don't explain such broad-based differences in pay for similar outcomes.

No matter how hard a woman works or how many credentials she earns, she will often be paid less than men with the same credentials producing the same outcomes.

So while the man who is working hard justifiably feels he is earning every penny of his pay, the fact that he is working hard for his pay doesn't justify the gender salary differential.

This raises several key points:

- The *permeability of barriers matters*. If a handful of token unprivileged are admitted to a privileged club for public relations purposes ("you see, we're not biased at all"), this is not the same as a truly merit-based, outcome-based system that is completely blind to gender, ethnicity, religion, age, etc.

  Exceptions do not prove the rule! A truly merit-based system generates *advantaged classes* that anyone with the requisite abilities, skills, experience and values can enter.

- *Unequal outcomes can still persist in a merit-based, outcome-based system*, for the reasons outlined above: innate abilities, family support, instilled values, better decisions and so on. But if the barrier is highly permeable, even individuals with unfavorable family backgrounds and a bit of good fortune can still work their way into the advantaged class via perseverance and a commitment to long-term goals, honesty and excellence. If the barriers are impermeable, no amount of good fortune or hard work will move the unprivileged into the privileged class.

How easy is it to join a particular class? Can anyone move into the class based on merit? It can be difficult to join an advantaged class (for example, the class of people who have earned STEM – science, technology, engineering, math -- PhDs), but if admission is based solely on merit and talent, this is still an equal opportunity for all. But if certain classes of individuals are not allowed admission regardless of their talent and merit, then that is evidence of impermeable privilege.

- People in privileged classes typically feel their advantages are earned, but this may reflect self-justification rather than reality. *Bush*

For example, consider the (male) student mentioned above who gains admission to an elite Ivy League university not on his merit but on the basis of his family's donations to the school. If he is a typical member of the moneyed elite, he can squeak by with poor grades, get his diploma and then step into a six-figure job based on his family connections.

While this individual may feel he earned his degree and well-paid position, the truth is that, stripped of privilege, he would never have been admitted on merit alone, nor would he have secured the high-paying job right out of college on merit alone.

Consider the well-documented phenomenon of *driving while black*: African-American drivers are pulled over by police far more often than drivers of other ethnicities. While each police patrol may have a reason for pulling over the driver of a particular vehicle that has nothing to do with the driver's race, statistically this explanation doesn't explain the disparity.

Regardless of what the African-American individual does in terms of merit or outcome, they remain African-American and are thus exposed to the risk of getting pulled over for *driving while black*.

The Anglo, Asian or Hispanic individual who does not get pulled over doesn't feel they have any special privilege; whatever the cause, the disparity is invisible to those who haven't been pulled over multiple times for reasons that may well boil down to suspicion and racial profiling.

This leads to a another important point about privilege:

- *-Only the unprivileged are in a position to see the differences between how the system treats the privileged and how the system treats the unprivileged, because only the unprivileged experience exclusion.*

The Role of Technology in Limiting Privilege and Bias

All this raises a question: what kind of system eliminates social privilege and opens equal opportunities to all?

The answer I describe in my book *A Radically Beneficial World* is technology-based: each member of every Community Labor Integrated Money Economy (CLIME) group is paid the same for every hour of work as every other member in the region. Every member and group has the same opportunity to buy and sell goods and services on their own in the CLIME marketplace. Different groups will earn different outcomes, but the opportunities for advancement will be equal for all participants, as individuals can switch groups, join multiple groups or start their own group.

Software, if properly programmed, is blind to human bias. A software-based system can eliminate bias and privilege by treating every member and organization equally.

Imagine a city in the near future that only allows self-driving rental cars on its streets: human-driven privately owned vehicles are banned as hazards. Every rented vehicle obeys all traffic rules, and accidents are rare. (Recall that vehicle speeds are low in congested cities.)

Why would the city waste valuable police time cruising streets filled with vehicles that cannot deviate from traffic rules? The only time it would make sense to send a traffic officer out is to file a report on the rare accident.

If an officer did pull a car over for a defective tail light, the driver would be blameless, as the responsibility for repairing the tail light would fall to the rental car agency, not the driver. Since the vehicles would record all activity, there would be readily available evidence if police officers pulled over vehicles with no ticketable defects because the driver happened to be African-American.

Not only would it make no sense financially for the city to pay police officers to monitor self-driving rental cars, any city government that persisted in *driving while black* bias would open itself to punishing civil lawsuits. The data collected by the rental car fleet would be undeniable in court.

Technology cannot eliminate human bias or poor decisions, but it has the potential to eliminate systemic bias and privilege, and collect data that makes any remaining bias transparent to all—not just to the unprivileged who experience the bias first-hand.

Technology has the potential to offer everyone the same opportunities for individually tailored advancement. While software cannot eliminate differences in wealth-based opportunities—for example, the children of wealthy families get private lessons, while the children of disadvantaged families do not—technology has the potential to level the playing field (by enabling nearly free lessons tailored to each student), provide transparency at levels that are unreachable in systems riddled with human bias.

While there is no substitute for caring, encouraging parents and mentors, technology can open the path to the advantaged class that is currently a thicket of obstacles for the disadvantaged.

Access to the Advantaged Class Is Path Dependent

We are now in a position to see that simply limiting privilege is not enough to move people from the disadvantaged class into the advantaged class. Ensuring the system offers equal opportunity to all does not give everyone equal access to the tools needed to pursue/take advantage of those opportunities.

The process of moving from the disadvantaged class to the advantaged class is *path dependent*: the process requires moving progressively from one step to the next, and acquiring the skills, experience and values needed to progress to the next step. IN other words, upward mobility is like a ladder: we don't move from the bottom rung to the top rung in one leap, we steadily climb the ladder one higher rung at a time.

We can illustrate path dependency by considering the different outcomes experienced by two equally bright children born into similarly disadvantaged circumstances of low household income, a dysfunctional family, latchkey parent, poor schooling, etc.

- Student One is accepted directly into an elite university without any preparation after graduating from high school. This student basically jumped from the first step to one near the top. Though the student is as smart as the other more advantaged students, he/she lacks the tools, experiences and values needed to excel in an elite university. For example, since the student's prior education was limited and his/her household was lacking in books and enrichment, many of the cultural/historical references that are essential to understanding advanced topics are unknown to the student. This student is unprepared not just intellectually, but in terms of the value set required to excel: self-discipline, ability to set long-term goals and sacrifice daily to reach these goals, collaborative social skills, the self-confidence needed to learn difficult material on one's own, and so on.

  Conversely, the other students who grew up in an advantaged household with sufficient income to fund enrichment classes, books and cultural experiences and parents who instilled these core values may be unaware of his/her advanced progression up these steps.

- Student Two is given the means to move from one step to the next in intellectual, cultural and values-based enrichment. When that student enters the elite university, it is not an alien landscape filled with references that are unknown, but a familiar environment of learning, collaboration, competition and advancement from one level of knowledge to the next.

The point here is that limiting privilege does not in itself open a pathway from disadvantaged class to advantaged class. We must lay those stepping stones to make an abstract opportunity into a concrete opportunity. It's not enough to open doors at the end of the path; since the journey to the advantaged class is path dependent, each step of the pathway must be accessible.

We can visualize this path dependency as the difference in outcomes between two equally healthy saplings. One is planted in a shallow, narrow hole in hardpan clay soil, and given no fertilizer or compost. Starved of nutrients and surrounded by hard clay, this sapling struggles to get the nutrients needed to stay alive, much less grow, *because there is no other likely outcome of this deprivation.*

The other sapling is planted in nutrient-rich deep soil and nurtured with plentiful compost and organic fertilizers. This sapling grows quickly *because there is no other likely outcome of this expansive, nurturing environment.*

To continue the analogy: tossing a handful of chemical fertilizer on the sapling struggling in the hardpan clay might give the plant a brief boost, but it won't change the outcome. The only way to change the outcome is to dig a large, deep hole in the clay and fill it with nutrient-rich soil and compost.

As I noted above, software cannot replace caring, encouraging parents and mentors, but it can automate some of the basic mentoring and connect mentors with those working their way from the disadvantaged class to the advantaged class.

In my book *Get a Job, Build a Real Career and Defy a Bewildering Economy*, I describe the eight essential skills required to move into the advantaged class. These are soft skills that anyone can acquire with the right effort, training and encouragement. Much of this path-dependent mentoring can be automated, if there is an institutional pathway that eliminates the obstacles posed by privilege.

The Difference between Unearned Privilege and Earned Advantages

As noted earlier, *privilege is the result of systems that are rigged in favor of the few at the expense of the many*. **Privilege is unearned, advantages are earned**. Privilege offloads accountability for outcomes and risk onto others, while securing the gains: that is the essence of a rigged system.

The privileged class avoids having skin in the game (i.e. risk of poor outcomes), while the advantaged class is required to have skin in the game.

For example, consider a corporate employee who earns a salary and stock options, which are options to buy the company's stock at a set price that is typically lower than the market price. A senior employee might earn 10,000 shares in stock options. This stock-option is a form of earned compensation, not privilege.

COMMON PRACTICE

Remember that privilege is not earned; it skims private wealth in a rigged system. Here's how financial privilege works. The privileged few at the top of the corporate pyramid first grant themselves millions of shares of stock options. Then they arrange for the company to borrow a billion dollars, which is used to buy back shares of the company's stock. This immense purchase boosts the value of the stock in two ways: the purchase reduces the number of outstanding shares, pushing the price-earnings ratio of the stock up, and the surging demand pushes prices higher.

500 MILLiON UNiTed HeaLTh

BoNuS

In effect, the privileged few use the corporation's borrowing power to personally enrich themselves. A merely advantaged salaried employee does not have the power to skim tens of millions of dollars in private wealth by leveraging the corporation's line of credit. Unlike a salaried position, the power to exploit stock buybacks is a form of privilege that is both low-risk and inaccessible to the merely advantaged.

The barrier between advantaged and privileged is not always impermeable. In a one-party system, for example, an unprivileged person could start as a low-level political functionary and slowly work his/her way to the top of the political hierarchy. Once in the top position, the official is the recipient of large bribes from property developers and corporations that require a government permit.

The official doesn't earn the bribes; they flow to whomever holds the office. He gets the bribes whether he is lazy or efficient. The position is privileged, and the individual holding the position reaps the benefits of the rigged system until he/she retires to sunny climes with a newly acquired hoard of private wealth.

The next functionary to hold the office will pocket the same stream of bribes.

There are several distinctions we can make between privileged positions/classes vs. the merely advantaged classes:

- **Merit has little influence in the privileged position.** The private wealth flowing to the office holder or top corporate manager is largely unaffected by the quality of his/her performance. Accountability is easily dodged; should questions arise, the functionary or CEO can step down and retire with his private wealth intact.
- *The friction of accountability and risk are reduced by privilege.* The unprivileged have to stand in line; the privileged get an exemption. The advantaged have accountability and performance reviews; the privileged do not. The advantaged class must jump through zoning and planning permit hoops; the privileged obtain expedited permits granted by the top echelon of political power.
- *The gains of privilege are asymmetrical.* The advantaged might earn 10,000 stock options after years of service to the corporation. The privileged can grant themselves 1,000,000+ stock options.
- *Process and position, not outcome, generate privileged private wealth.* The political functionary isn't exposed to the risks of a development

project that fails; he collects his substantial bribe without any exposure to the risks of the project failing. As long as the functionary issues the permit, the outcome has no impact on his private wealth.

The CEO who orders stock buybacks to boost his private wealth keeps his new wealth even if the corporation falters after he leaves office.

As a general rule, privilege is maintained by *process and position*. Outcomes are intrinsically risky—they can be good or bad. Privilege avoids risk and accountability by relying on procedures and the authority of position to secure wealth and power.

Privilege Is PORR

As noted in the Introduction, privilege is a *specific arrangement of power, opportunity, responsibility and risk (PORR)*. There are any number of such arrangements, but each rigs the game for a privileged class.

I have already described three specific examples of such arrangements: corporate managers who skim great private wealth off stock buybacks; political offices that skim great wealth via bribes paid to the office holder, and the child of wealthy alumni who gains privileged access to admission at an elite university.

Another example is public union government employees, who receive benefits from membership in a privileged class that are not available to the unprivileged private-sector work force: permanent employment (i.e. they cannot be fired except in extreme conditions); generous pension and healthcare benefits that are unavailable in the private sector, a no-skin-in-the-game environment of following process/procedure rather than being accountable for outcomes, and the unparalleled security of using the government's ability to raise taxes to pay their salaries and benefits.

These privileges flow directly from membership, not merit or positive outcomes. Members of this class who perform poorly receive the same pay and benefits as those who produce outstanding outcomes, with minor variations due to seniority and credentialing.

Conversely, an economy without privilege requires every participant to have *skin in the game*, i.e. be exposed to risk and be accountable for outcomes. In an economy without privilege:

- *process is subservient to outcomes*; and

- everyone has equal opportunity to join an advantaged class that doesn't protect its members from accountability and risk (instead, it rewards those who accept risk and responsibility for outcomes).

Many of us are in classes that we don't recognize as privileged because only the unprivileged experience the insecurity, risk and diminished opportunities that we don't experience because our privilege protects us from those negatives.

Our default setting is to assert that our position, membership, pay and benefits are all earned. But as noted above, the fact that we are performing labor doesn't mean we aren't the recipient of rewards that are not paid to others doing the exact same work in the same career slot.

The permeability of the barrier between classes does not negate privilege. For example, the claim that anyone can become a State employee overlooks the fact that the State funds itself off the wages and taxes paid by the private sector. Roughly 20% of the work force can work for the State, but the other 80% must find work in the largely unprivileged private sector.

Though the rewards of privilege vary, *privilege is ethically scale-invariant*: all privilege is ethically equivalent. We cannot claim that some types of privilege are acceptable and others are unacceptable. To do is to claim the right to preserve our privileges at the expense of others while denying others the same exclusive control of a rigged game.

In an economy without privilege, *power, opportunity, responsibility and risk are all equally available and everyone is equally exposed to outcomes*. In such an economy, power (such as being elected to an office) is always temporary and contingent upon the consent of the governed.

Chapter Two - Privilege, Inequality and Poverty

We are now in a position to better appreciate that *the only possible outcome of privilege is rising inequality and poverty*, and the only possible outcome of rising inequality is social instability that leads to collapse of the status quo.

Let's start by recalling that privilege is functionally equivalent to autocracy. We can actually extend this and say that privilege is functionally equivalent to oligarchy (the rule of the few), monopoly (where the few control the engines of *value creation*) and *neofeudalism*, which I define as a *mode of production dominated by credit-based, leveraged capital* in which the majority are *debt-serfs* and the financial nobility with access to cheap, unlimited credit own the vast majority of productive assets.

Privilege involves controlling access to the engines of wealth/value creation: rigged games, low-interest credit, secure employment, and opportunities to leverage financial, social and intellectual capital to reap the wealth from productive assets. In essence, privilege means *risk-free access to the economy's gains*. The privileged few secure most of the gains, leaving little for the unprivileged many. last TAX CUT

This is precisely what we currently see in the United States and many other nations. The top 5% have reaped most of the gains in wealth and income while the wealth and income of the bottom 95% has stagnated (or even declined, when adjusted for inflation) for decades.

To better understand why inequality and poverty are the only possible outcome of privilege, we need to understand the sources of poverty.

What Is Poverty?

That poverty is the lack of the material necessities of life is self-evident. The problem with this definition of poverty is that it naturally leads to the idea that the solution to poverty is to give people either material necessities and/or money to buy them. But this transfer is not a systemic solution to poverty, for it is based on a faulty understanding of poverty.

To understand poverty, we must first understand that an economy can be distilled down to two systems: *ownership of income streams and the distribution of those income streams*. Income flows from productive assets, i.e. the *engines of wealth/value creation*. Net income is simply the surplus between the cost of production (the inputs) and the value of what has been produced (the output).

There are various means of distributing this net income to participants in the economy: wages paid by owners of an income stream, income earned by individuals who own an engine of wealth, profits paid as dividends by owners of income streams, and wages paid by the State (i.e. government) from tax revenues collected from private income.

Productivity is a measure of how much output is generated from inputs. While there are various measures of wealth, the kind of wealth that matters in solving poverty are the engines of wealth that can be made more productive with investment, knowledge and innovation.

If we imagine the wealth in a pirate's treasure chest—gold coins, precious stones, etc.—we find that this wealth is based on the relative scarcity of the items, not on their productivity. The precious stones are inert and do not generate goods and services. The productivity of precious stones is zero. These scarce items can act as money, but outside of an economy that generates and distributes income, their value is decorative.

In contrast, farmland and tools are productive assets, i.e. engines of wealth. The inputs of capital (land, tools, etc.) and labor yield an output with an economic value. Productive innovations leverage the inputs into higher yields. This increases the income and thus the value of the system of production.

This brief overview enables us to discern the systemic outlines of poverty: Economies with large surpluses but highly uneven distribution of the surplus will have relatively few very wealthy people and a much larger mass of poor people.

So what makes the distribution of income uneven? There are two basic dynamics:

1) the ownership of productive assets (the engines of wealth) is highly concentrated in a few powerful hands, or
2) the State harvests most of the economy's surplus and distributes it to a small circle of politically powerful cronies.

In other words, poverty is the result of a highly asymmetric distribution of income from an equally asymmetric allocation of political power and productive capital.

We have seen that whenever ownership of the engines of wealth creation is concentrated in the hands of a few, the inevitable result is poverty. And if the State has unlimited power to expropriate private income streams, the result is highly unequal distribution of wealth as the State's insiders scoop up the wealth.

Thus solving poverty distills down to (a) *distributing new capital to disadvantaged households and their communities, and (b) then boosting the productivity of that capital.*

This leads to two profound conclusions:

1) To solve poverty, ownership of the engines of wealth creation must be broadly distributed as *new capital,* and
2) The income generated by this broad ownership must be beyond the reach of an oligarchic State of entrenched cronies.

A systemic solution to poverty therefore has two parts: widely distribute the tools to build productive capital, and encourage innovation that boosts the productivity of those broadly distributed engines of wealth creation.

Historically, redistributive schemes to reduce poverty simply call for taking productive capital away from one person and giving it to another person. That these schemes fail is self-evident. A better, systemic solution to poverty is to distribute *new capital*—capital that has been created by the work and innovation of newly enfranchised owners.

As we see on a daily basis, technology is enabling the low-cost distribution of *digital (intangible) capital* that enables other forms of productive capital.

Tangible capital can be confiscated by the State. But *intangible capital* is less accessible, especially if it is distributed and held in highly decentralized and encrypted forms.

A just, transparently governed State will naturally earn the trust of its citizenry who will then voluntarily pay taxes to support the State's functions. But poverty is not associated with just, transparently governed states; it is associated with exploitive autocracies, oligarchies and monopolies/cartels dominated by parasitic, privileged elites. Poverty is permanent unless income-producing capital can be held by individuals, households and communities in forms that cannot be easily confiscated by a State that enforces the privileges of the few at the expense of the many.

The Root of Inequality: Lack of Capital and Secure Paid Work

Economist John Kenneth Galbraith concluded that mass poverty was caused by a lack of capital and technical expertise—what we call *intangible capital*—and the fatalism of the impoverished, whose efforts are systemically stymied by centralized power centers. He saw physical mobility as the one proven way out of mass poverty, and indeed, this dynamic has fueled what is likely the greatest migration in human history from rural areas to urban areas—a migration that continues to this day.

But migration has its limits. Not everyone is free to move to more prosperous urban areas, and the vast majority of transplanted rural residents are still mired in endemic poverty within sprawling urban slums and shantytowns.

Migration alone does not provide what Galbraith identified as essential: capital, expertise and a social infrastructure that enables escape from a resigned acceptance of poverty—what some call *learned helplessness*.

Secure paid work can only arise from a foundation of productive capital, which includes technical expertise, money and the *symbolic capital* of an organizational structure that is independent of autocracies, monopolies and other structures that enforce privilege.

The Eight Types of Capital

The taxonomy of capital has been outlined in many different ways, but most list variations of these eight basic types of capital. The most important division is between *tangible capital* such as tools and natural resources and *intangible capital*, which I broadly define as *best practices* that leverage the productive potential of material capital.

In a digital analogy, tangible wealth can be thought of as the *hardware* while intangible wealth is the *software*.

Material wealth (1 through 3) includes:

1. **Financial capital**: money in cash, marketable investments, etc.
2. **Natural capital**: the resources of the natural world including living capital (fish, trees, etc.) and resources such as minerals and fossil fuels.
3. **Fixed capital**: machinery, tools, communications networks, etc.

Intangible wealth (4 through 8) includes:

4. **Human capital**: the intellectual and experiential capital needed to make the other forms of capital productive.
5. **Social capital**: the connections and relationships that enable productive collaboration and cooperation.
6. **Cultural capital**: the political and social institutions that enable broad-based increases in productivity.

Note: Some may view my final two types of capital—*symbolic* and *infrastructure*—as being part of cultural and fixed capital, but I see them as distinct forms of capital.

7. **Symbolic capital** describes the conceptual tools that enable new ways of being productive. The concept of credit is an example of symbolic capital, because without the conceptual tools of collateral, amortization and interest, this form of financial capital could not exist. The open-source software movement is another example of symbolic capital; so is the crowd-sourcing model of solving problems or raising money. While cultural capital may be confined to specific cultures, symbolic capital, being conceptual in nature, is more likely to migrate across borders.
8. **Infrastructure capital** is the system that results when all the other forms of capital work hand in hand. One way to illustrate infrastructure capital is to imagine a self-made billionaire being dropped into a desert in a nation with essentially no fixed capital and populated by nomadic peoples who have no interaction with the global market economy. Our billionaire's wealth, skills, knowledge and social capital would have no value there, because the infrastructure that supports these forms of capital is lacking.

Using Capital to Create an Infrastructure of Opportunity

Only the sum total of all the various forms of capital can create a universally accessible *infrastructure of opportunity*.

If privilege dominates the system and there is no mobility of labor and capital, no transparent markets for labor and capital, no creative destruction of corrupt systems, no decentralized access to credit, few means of cooperation, weak rule of law and property rights, little room for innovation, and no understanding of the essential role of risk, opportunities are innately scarce.

Virtually all efforts made in such an environment will be lost because it's a desert for broad-based opportunity.

Conversely, when there are productive incentives, transparent markets for labor, capital and credit, mobility of labor and capital, abundant ways to cooperate with others, creative destruction of privilege and cronyism, strong rule of law and property rights, and an appetite for innovation and risk, opportunities are broad-based.

This is one reason why cities offer so many more opportunities than rural areas: cities offer more access to credit, mobility of labor and capital, more opportunities for innovation to take root, and so on.

We can best understand the leverage provided by intangible capital by comparing the productivity of similarly skilled rural migrants doing construction work in the U.S. vs. South America. Semi-literate migrants working in the U.S. construction industry are four times more productive than those laboring in South America. even though the materials, tools and skill level of the workers are roughly equal. The difference is the practices developed and incentivized by the intangible capital in the U.S.

When we speak of eliminating privilege, what we are really talking about is building a universally accessible *infrastructure of opportunity* so those currently trapped in the disadvantaged class can build a sustainable prosperity with their own labor, capital and resources.

Poverty: Not Just Material

Our natural first focus in alleviating poverty is on the material necessities of life. But this focus on material necessities blinds us to the intangible sources of poverty and the critical roles of work and being productive socially (i.e. having a meaningful social role) - not just for wealth-building, but also for one's overall feeling of well-being.

The reductionist idea that simply transferring money to the poor will alleviate poverty has paradoxically and tragically led to enduring pathologies of poverty in which the poor have few opportunities to gain autonomy, dignity, self-worth, meaning, membership, pride, sense of purpose, and participation in organizations that build ownership of productive capital. While many people still see guaranteed income issued by the State as a solution to poverty, this scheme reduces the poor to dependent, atomized consumers who have no work, opportunity or capital - and thus no sources of dignity, self-worth, meaning, membership, pride and purpose.

Providing the material necessities but stripping away the social, psychological and spiritual necessities of human life is cruel and immoral. Rather than being beneficial, social welfare is intrinsically pathological.

The only systemic solution to poverty is to offer universal opportunities to become valued producers, not dependent, marginalized consumers stripped of capital and purpose. In other words, the systemic solution to poverty is to offer stable paid work for all within an organization that provides incentives, democratized work places, and accountability while serving the needs of the larger community.

Material sufficiency amidst a poverty of meaningful social roles generates a host of self-destructive pathologies, and conventional poverty-alleviation programs are blind to this perverse consequence of *social poverty*. Human beings need positive social roles as much as they need shelter and food. We can understand this on an individual level by asking: what sort of positive personal narrative is available to people who have little autonomy and are dependent on the State? What sources of pride and purpose are available to them?

Any systemic solution to poverty must make it easy for all participants to construct a positive personal narrative. This means that the system must offer a wealth of opportunities for meaningful participation, pride, purpose, the accumulation of capital, security, self-worth and dignity.

Social Defeat, Behavioral Sinks, Positive Social Roles and Public Happiness

We cannot truly understand poverty unless we understand the psychosocial pathologies that arise from loss of autonomy, financial dependence and the absence of a social order that (a) provides an abundance of positive social roles, and (b) values the common good and *public happiness* above the maximization of individual wealth (i.e. privilege).

Financial dependence and the absence of a productive social order yield one output: *social defeat*, which I define as the surrender of autonomy, declining social status and a permanent State of insecurity and anxiety. Stripped of sources of dignity, self-worth, meaning, membership, pride, and purpose, the socially defeated slide into a shared hopelessness that researcher John B. Calhoun labeled a *behavioral sink*: as social roles erode and cease to function, self-reinforcing social pathologies escalate to the point of breakdown. This black hole of self-inflicted suffering is characterized by self-destructive mental states and behaviors such as chronic anxiety, resignation, domestic violence, self-medication with addictive substances, loss of empathy, the polarities of passivity and rage, and a spectrum of mental disorders from narcissism to attention deficit traits (ADT) to anti-social behaviors.

Social orders that excel in creating and distributing *social defeat* will necessarily be populated with unhappy, depressed, anxious and frustrated people, regardless of the material goods they possess.

One aspect of social defeat is the emptiness we experience when prosperity does not deliver the promised sense of fulfillment. A recent sociological study compared wealthy Hong Kong residents' sense of contentment with those of the immigrant maids who serve the moneyed elites. The study found that the maids were much happier than their wealthy employers, who were often suicidal and depressed. The maids, on the other hand, enjoyed membership in a trustworthy group – other maids they met with on their one day off – and a strong sense of purpose provided by their ongoing financial support of their families back home.

Social defeat is more pervasive and destructive than material want, as it cannot be solved with simple distributions of cash, the conventional solution to poverty that actually exacerbates social defeat. The only way to combat social defeat and the resulting behavioral sink is to resuscitate an *internally coherent social order* that offers a variety of positive social roles that restore autonomy and agency (i.e. the ability to make choices) to all participants.

The two types of conventional organizational models that excel at providing this *structure of purpose* are corporations and the armed forces. While the armed forces are based on duty and a rigid hierarchy of command, the corporation is based on private ownership, profit and a hierarchy of command.

To design an ideal *unit of social order*, we must reach beyond these conventional models and ask: what *internally coherent social order* will generate what author Garry Wills called *public happiness*?

Public happiness is not just the aggregation of individual happiness; it is a reflection of the social order's success in enabling the common good, one expression of which is the potential for individual fulfillment within organizations that serve the common good.

To understand the centrality of the common good to human fulfillment, we must consider the social traits that benefited humans during our 100,000 years as hunter-gatherers. What traits would natural selection place a premium on? Cooperation in productive work, sacrifice in service to the survival of the group, celebrating windfalls with communal consumption, leadership based on strength, success and wisdom. My colleague Bart Dessart describes this dynamic as "interacting meaningfully with most other people around them. Meaningful interaction means doing things for each other, relying on each other, and at times taking risks for each other."

How Poverty and Privilege are Related

Poverty is not just material want or lack of work. It is a systemic scarcity of purpose, meaningful opportunities to contribute and communities that provide the sources of well-being.

Privilege restricts the pathways from the disadvantaged class to the advantaged class by imposing *rentier fees* on the economy that impoverish the many to the benefit of the few. Rentier fees do not add value; they simply divert income from the many to the few. *TRickLe dowN*

Expanding the private wealth of the privileged classes at the expense of the unprivileged does not create public happiness. Instead, it sows inequality and instability that destroy the possibility of public happiness.

In diverting capital and resources to itself, the privileged class starves the system of the resources needed to widen the pathway from disadvantage to advantage. In this way, the multiple pathologies of poverty are the inescapable consequence of privilege.

Privilege Generates Corruption, Injustice and Stagnation

Privilege corrupts societies, organizations and economies by rewarding those who didn't earn their position and excluding those who would have earned the position had it been based solely on merit. Privilege is functionally equivalent to a corrupt system in which the few demand bribes of the many to go about their business.

Cartels and monopolies are functionally equivalent to forced bribery, as they set the price above what it would be in a free market. The difference between the market price and what cartels/monopolies charge is in effect a forced bribe—a *rentier fee* that goes directly to the privileged. This corruption erodes both the social order and the economy. By rewarding privilege rather than merit, risk and innovation, the system incentivizes accumulating private wealth by any means.

Making the private accumulation of wealth the highest goal decays the foundations of the social order in a number of ways: it erodes fairness, social cohesion and opens a gulf between classes that diminishes a shared sense of purpose—all essential elements of stable social orders.

By diverting money from the many to the few, privilege deprives the many of their income and capital - in effect concentrating wealth in the hands of the few. Once wealth is concentrated, it distorts markets (for example, with stock buybacks) and further expands the wealth of the privileged elites: the rich get richer because they own the engines of wealth creation.

Thus privilege doesn't simply act as a *rentier fee* on the economy; it also corrupts the social/political order and capital markets and drains the economy of the essential and intrinsically disruptive forces of social mobility, innovation and competition. This corruption deprives individuals of opportunity—what we might call direct, concrete consequences—and parasitically bleeds the economy of vitality.

The privileged person who gets the high-paying job not on merit but for being an insider deprives a more qualified unprivileged person of the job he/she would have won on merit alone. This hurts the individual deprived of the secure job, and also hurts the economy in a systemic way, as the privileged incompetent are a dead weight on productivity. The money that could have been invested in fostering talent and innovation is siphoned off to overpay the incompetent privileged and *rentier fees to privileged classes*.

If we add up these costs, both to individuals denied opportunity and to the economy as a whole, we see that the *only possible output of privilege is injustice and stagnation*. An economy dominated by the economic privileged (monopolies and cartels) and a political oligarchy is an economy which suppresses competition and innovation because these forces threaten to disrupt the rigged games of the privileged few. *The only possible outcome of suppressing competition and innovation is stagnation of the entire economy*, an enormous cost that is ultimately paid by everyone, including the privileged.

The social cost of corruption and injustice is difficult to measure but is nonetheless real and devastating to social cohesion, shared sense of purpose and social mobility. Privilege can only exist if the status quo enforces it, and the unprivileged bear the bitter fruit: injustice and inequality.

At some point, the unprivileged realize the corrupt system is no longer worth supporting, and the status quo collapses.

Negative Economic Impacts of Privilege

By definition, privilege enforces inequality: the privileged push risk and accountability onto the unprivileged and siphon off the economy's wealth/value for themselves. This structural inequality imposed by privilege has only one possible output: *poverty*, because the capital and opportunity that would have otherwise flowed to the unprivileged in an economy free of privilege get diverted to the privileged classes.

Privilege generates poverty by weakening the economy structurally, diminishing its productivity and its potential to adapt effectively to rapidly changing circumstances.

Privilege weakens the economy in several ways:

- It channels most of the economy's gains into the hands of a few, leaving less available to the many.
- It suppresses innovation and competition via regulatory capture and other means.
- It leads to stagnation as capital is siphoned off to serve the narrow interests of the privileged classes rather than the economy as a whole.
- Since the path from the disadvantaged to the advantaged class doesn't serve the narrow interests, it is starved of capital and resources.
- As the status quo is dominated by the privileged, the resources of the system are devoted to protecting the privileged from risk and disruption. This protection saps the economy of the flexibility needed to invest in enterprises that would undermine the monopolies of the privileged.

In summary, privilege is a dead weight on the economy that siphons off the capital and suppresses the flexibility needed to remain productive as global competition increases and physical resources dwindle. The economy ossifies and stagnates, distributing impoverishment - the only possible outcome of privilege.

The causal connection between privilege and poverty is often masked by two dynamics:

(1) the promise that the unprivileged can become privileged if they work hard enough; and

(2) the belief that the unprivileged are actually benefiting from the status quo.

Trickle down

In a rising tide of prosperity, the evil consequences of privilege are masked by the impression that *a rising tide raises all boats*. The status quo actually goes all out to promote any metrics which support this (mis)perception. The people earning $100 more a month are happy with their lot, especially if everyone else in their cohort/class seems to be enjoying a similar level of rising prosperity. This perception nurtures a sense that the system benefits everyone, not just a few.

The asymmetric gains of the privileged are unseen by the unprivileged, who are typically unaware of the sweetheart contracts, double-dipping, bribery (often cloaked as campaign contributions or philanthropy to politically powerful foundations), stock buybacks and other rigged games that benefit the privileged at levels unimaginable to the average wage earner.

Studies have found that prosperity and poverty are relative rather than absolute: two people with the same income may have widely divergent perceptions of their wealth. As social animals, we cue our perceptions to what we see in our group/tribe. If a few people in our social circle are making $1,000 more a month, our $100 in extra income pales by comparison and so we feel poor relative to these more prosperous colleagues. But if everyone we know is making about $100 more a month, and we don't see the privileged few making $100,000 more a month, we still feel wealthier, even if the financial reality is the majority of gains are flowing to the few, not the many.

This is precisely what has taken place since the 2008 financial crisis. According to economist Emmanuel Saez, 95% of all income gains from 2009 to 2012 flowed to the top 1%. Apologists were quick to point out that the top 1% had lost more money than the bottom 99% in the meltdown, but this overlooks the vast wealth acquired by the 1% in the previous 15 years and the staggering gains in assets such as stocks, bonds and real estate reaped by the 1% since 2009.

All of this changes once the unprivileged see their disposable income stagnating while the wealth of the privileged continues soaring. Rather than feeling that they are participating in rising prosperity, the unprivileged finally figure out that the system is rigged in favor of the privileged few. A sense of injustice and class division dismantles the "rising tide raises all boats" confidence in the system, and the unprivileged lose faith in the social and political order.

The same disillusionment manifests when those who work their way up to the advantaged class realize that no amount of hard work will crack open the doors to the privileged class.

Societies require social cohesion and shared purpose to endure. When the privileged sacrifice more for the common good than the unprivileged, social cohesion is maintained: though the benefits of the social order flow asymmetrically to the privileged class, so too do the costs and sacrifices. Put another way: *the pain has to be equal*, otherwise resentment will rise and social cohesion will be lost.

But when the privileged class siphons off the benefits while sacrificing little for the common good, social cohesion erodes and the social order is doomed to instability and collapse.

Chapter Three - Privilege and Our Mode of Production

Privilege manifests in the financial, social and political realms. The three are intertwined: wealth generates social and political privilege; family connections open doors to political and financial power; and political power leads to social connections and opportunities to accumulate private wealth.

To understand how privilege is woven into the fabric of our social order, we need to understand society as a complex ecosystem of cultural, political and financial dynamics. This ecosystem is our *mode of production*, which we will explore in this chapter.

The Economy, Society and Governance: One System

Academic specialization has subdivided what is essentially indivisible—a society with cultural, economic and political characteristics—into the separate fields of economics, sociology and political science. While there are self-evident reasons to specialize—expertise in a wide field is no longer attainable, and efficiency is best served by narrow expertise—this institutionalized specialization has crippled our *integrated understanding* of the whole.

Conventional economics is effectively detached from cultural, social and political realities, as if finance and economics exist in a separate world. Few economists study the impact of markets on culture or society, or the economic impacts of widespread political corruption. Fewer still question the role of central banking in generating inequality, or the role of privilege in creating inequality and social instability.

Each specialty is bound by convention to remain safely corralled in its paddock, lest breaking down barriers devalues each fiefdom's area of expertise. Each avoids unpleasant pressure from large donors and funding sources by ignoring potentially disruptive topics. Those within each field are akin to members of a priesthood that severely punishes those who stray by limiting jobs, prestige and visibility to those who stay safely in the assigned paddocks. This ostracizing of dissent is carefully cloaked; only those who don't openly question the orthodoxies of their sponsoring institutions rise to positions of power.

This process includes *self-censorship*, where those who question the viability and morality of the current world-system know to keep their doubts private, lest they lose their place on the bureaucratic or academic ladder.

The career-ending consequence of questioning the ruling orthodoxy is not limited to the social sciences; it is an inherent feature of hierarchical institutions, from the Armed Forces to the Forest Service.

Playing it safe has left the institutionalized specialties incapable of a truly integrated analysis of the economic-social-political whole.

There is another factor that limits their ability to make sense of the profound changes that are unfolding. The social sciences' longstanding envy of hard science's mathematical supremacy has led to an over-compensatory obsession with collecting and analyzing data, as if massaging data is all that's needed to turn economics into a hard science. But since economics, sociology and political science all deal with human behavior and internal states—goals, beliefs, motivations and values—they are intrinsically more akin to psychology than physics. There is a place for data, but equation-driven models alone are not enough to construct an integrated understanding of a society that is not an economic machine but a highly dynamic ecosystem.

What we choose to measure limits our understanding of complex systems. Our choice of what to measure defines our conclusions, and this reality makes data-driven analyses especially prone to selective blindness: we no longer see what we're not measuring, and we certainly don't act on what we don't measure.

These realities leave conventional specialties poorly prepared to understand that *privilege is the engine of inequality* or the enormity of the technological advances that are disrupting society and the economy.

We will lose our way if we do not keep in mind that the *economy, society and governance are indivisible*.

The Taxonomy of Privilege

To tease apart the many manifestations of privilege, we must construct a *taxonomy of privilege*.

- Birthright: privileges that come with being born into a privileged class, caste, tribe, gender
- Wealth: the ability to create and distribute currency (money) and credit

- Wealth: ownership of income producing assets
- Wealth: monopoly or cartel control that guarantees profits
- Wealth: access to low-cost credit which can be used to buy productive assets
- Political power: leveraging the power of the State to enforce private privileges
- Political patronage: obtaining privileges by serving political elites
- Politically protected membership (guilds, unions, etc.)
- Bureaucratic privilege: being rewarded for process rather than outcome
- Social/Cultural privilege: access to influential people and social capital

What stands out in this taxonomy is the dominance of wealth/finance. To understand why, we need to understand the nature of our *mode of production*.

Our Mode of Production: Centralized, Industrialized, Globalized, Financialized, Networked, Fossil-Fuel Dependent, Neo-feudal and Neo-liberal

What is a *mode of production*? A mode of production combines *productive forces* (financial capital, labor, tools, buildings, technologies, knowledge, natural resources and improved land) and the *social aspects of production* (social, legal and political systems).

Everyone living in a mode of production assumes there is no other way to relate to the material world and other people other than the way they do so. But in fact there are many ways to relate to the natural world and to other people.

Though we divide the social and economic orders, the concept of *modes of production* helps us understand that the two are one system: our society is the result of economic and social constructs that organize and limit both the economy and society.

In the context of this analysis, privilege is both economic and social, and the only way to limit privilege is to understand the structures that foster and enforce it.

What characterizes our current mode of production? It is:

- *centralized* (controlled by central governments and banks that hold monopolies on power and money),

- *industrialized* on a global scale (production and labor are commoditized),
- *financialized* (dependent on the processes of finance—debt, leverage and multiple financial instruments),
- *networked* (dependent on flows of information and feedback loops) and
- *dependent on fossil fuels* (only about 3% of total global energy consumption is generated by alternative renewable energy sources).

I have long argued that this mode of production is fundamentally *neofeudal*, meaning that the few at the top of the power/wealth pyramid benefit at the expense of the many. In effect, the current structure of State-finance-capitalism is an updated version of the old feudal model of landed nobility skimming rentier wealth from serfs!

In our modern version, the employed 'serfs' are indebted, socially fragmented and politically powerless, and the rentier skim is based on the asymmetry of credit/debt (hence my use of the term *debt-serfs*): the privileged financial elites use credit to buy productive assets, while the great mass of debt-serfs use credit to fund their consumption. The wealthy have access to low-cost credit which expands their ownership and income, while debt-serfs only have access to high-cost credit which makes them poorer by reducing their disposable income.

This is the result of the dominance of *finance capital* over *industrial capital*: State-cartels such as banking, healthcare and higher education enforce pricing that extracts profits by limiting competition, and foster a dependence on debt (for housing, higher education and consumption) that effectively enforces a financial servitude on debtors.

In this neofeudal mode of production, central banking delivers newly created capital into the hands of the few who then buy political influence (a.k.a. regulatory capture) and outbid those lacking access to cheap capital to take ownership of *value creation* in the economy.

The political capture secures protection from competition while ownership of value creation generates the income needed to buy protection. This State-cartel marriage creates a *cycle of expanding wealth/power for those who already own the wealth and have access to cheap credit.*

In this system, power and wealth inevitably accumulate at the top of the wealth-power pyramid, and inequality rises accordingly. In terms of systems analysis, *there is no other possible output of this mode of production other than rising inequality.*

This neofeudal mode of production is supported by a *neoliberal* set of values drawn from *game theory*: markets exist to maximize narrow self-interest and payoffs to participants, and these markets are the most efficient way to allocate capital and labor. This neoliberal view gives unparalleled advantages to mobile capital that can move easily around the world, exploiting resources, cheap labor and poorly regulated markets to serve neoliberalism's sole goal of *maximizing private gain by any means available.*

Privilege maximizes private gain by protecting the low-risk rentier skims of the few at the expense of the many.

These neoliberal values and mechanisms corrupt the political process, dissolve social cohesion (defined as the shared purpose that binds the various classes into a unified society) and distort the allocation of capital with perverse incentives.

Centralized Hierarchies Are Bastions of Privilege

How do the privileged enforce their rentier skims? By using centralized hierarchies, which enforce privilege. It would be impossible to do so in a decentralized economy. Imagine trying to impose your private privileges on a thousand separate city-states and a thousand different banks; the task is essentially impossible unless you centralize all these decentralized nodes by conquest into one centrally controlled hierarchy that can impose its will on every city-State and bank.

Privilege is only possible in centralized hierarchies. In opt-in, voluntary decentralized networks, *privilege is contingent*: it is granted for a limited period of time with the understanding that the privileged will work on behalf of the entire network. In systems-analysis terms, this is how democracy functions: leaders are elected for limited terms, so the privileges of power are granted for a specific length of time. This privilege is contingent on the elected official working diligently on behalf of the entire community/network. If the elected official pursues his/her own self-interest to the detriment of the electorate, he/she will soon be stripped of the privileges of power.

Our current mode of production is highly centralized, and dominated by rigid hierarchies of State and financial power. Eliminating privilege in such a system is essentially impossible, as the centralized hierarchies have the power to enforce their privileged status on an unwilling populace.

The only way to systemically eliminate privilege is to change the mode of production from centralized hierarchies that defend privilege to decentralized networks of opt-in localized participation. This is the mode of production I describe in my book *A Radically Beneficial World*.

Finance Dominates Our Mode of Production and Political Order

The taxonomy of privilege reflects the dominance of finance in our mode of production and political order, where those with financial privilege can buy political power, which is used to protect private privileges. We cannot understand the role of privilege in creating inequality unless we fully grasp the way financial privileges are created and enforced.

Chapter Four - The Nature of Financial Privilege

Our "Some Are More Equal Than Others" Financial System

Our mode of production generates inequality as a result of our *"some are more equal than others"* financial system. This structure is easy to understand, though those who benefit from it attempt to obfuscate its simple dynamics with intentionally confusing complexity.

The structure is simple: those who are closest to central bank credit-money spigots can borrow money at much lower rates than everyone else and as a result they will become wealthy at the expense of everyone else paying higher interest.

Why is this so? Because those who can borrow essentially unlimited sums at near-zero rates can outbid the rest of us paying much higher rates for *income streams, i.e. the engines of value creation*. These include rental housing, mines, factories, dividend-producing companies, high-yield debt, etc.

Since their carrying costs (i.e. the cost of servicing debt) are so much lower than those of everyone else, the net profits generated by the *engines of value creation* they bought with cheap credit are high. These profits serve as collateral for additional waves of borrowing and income-producing asset purchases, which drive a never-ending upward spiral of profits.

Access to cheap credit is therefore a self-reinforcing cycle: the more money you can borrow at low rates to buy income-producing assets, the more income and collateral you assemble to support additional borrowing to buy even more income-producing assets.

The highest-return investment is buying political influence over the regulations and tax policies that control income streams and assets. A relatively modest sum in campaign contributions and lobbying can lower regulatory and tax burdens by hundreds of millions of dollars. There is no equivalently high return available in the private marketplace.

The structure of our financial system is simple: banks and financiers can borrow nearly unlimited sums from the central bank, which can create unlimited sums out of thin air. Banks can leverage each dollar of cash into $20 in new loans. This is new money, and the bank earns interest on this newly created money. (We will discuss this system in greater depth shortly.)

The only possible output of such a system is that *some are more equal than others*, and those few who are more equal become immensely wealthy at the expense of the many.

This system cannot help but result in inequality and poverty. There is no other possible outcome.

We can see this in the difference between how the financially privileged and the unprivileged use credit. *The financially privileged use credit to buy productive assets* that generate additional income while *the unprivileged use credit to consume*: auto loans, student loans, credit cards etc. The wealthy use their cheap credit to buy value-creating, income-producing assets, while the unprivileged are stripped of their income by debt taken on to consume goods and services.

In George Orwell's famous novel *1984*, a purportedly egalitarian system was actually a highly asymmetric system of enforced privilege in which *some are more equal than others*. That describes our current system of financial privilege perfectly.

The only way to change our some are more equal than others system is to change the way money and credit are created and distributed.

The Role of Central Banks and Private Banks in Financial Privilege

The sole sources of credit in the modern world are central banks and private banks. Central banks, though nominally independent, are part of the State.

Central banks also offer lines of credit to private banks. Should private lending freeze up in a financial panic, the central bank stands ready to act as the *lender of last resort*.

The current monetary system is based on fractional reserve lending: private banks can issue a new loan of $100 (in effect, new money) backed by a mere $5 cash deposit in the bank. This ratio of $20 in new money issued on $1 in cash is common.

This system is based on the idea that banks will lend prudently, and that only 1 in 100 loans will go sour and result in losses to the bank. If one loan in 100 causes a $1 loss to the bank, the bank's cash declines from $5 to $4. But this loss is easily made up by the interest earned on the 99 loans that are still in good standing as long as the borrowers continue to pay interest and principal.

The problem in fractional reserve lending is obvious: should the bank miscalculate the creditworthiness of its borrowers, or if a financial crisis wipes out many of the borrowers' ability to service their loans, the bank could lose not $1 but $6. Since the bank only holds $5 in cash, the $6 loss renders the bank insolvent: it no longer has cash to refund depositor's money or fund new loans.

Economist Steve Keen has described the somewhat counterintuitive way money is withdrawn from this fractional reserve lending system as follows: when loans are paid off, the money created by the loan is subtracted from the supply of money. This is different from the intuitive idea that money doesn't just pop in and out of existence—for example, when you loan me $100 and I pay the $100 back to you, the money is still in circulation. Instead, in fractional reserve lending, when you pay the bank the $100 it created when it loaned you the $100, the $100 is no longer in circulation. And if the borrower of the $100 loan from the bank defaults, the bank must write off the $100 loan. Once again, the $100 is no longer in circulation. All money that is borrowed into existence vanishes from circulation when it is paid back or written off.

Conversely, private bank lending can create great sums of money--money that isn't issued by the State or its central bank or borrowed into existence. This money can be spent or invested wisely, or it can be squandered.

To illustrate the difference, imagine a small isolated kingdom.

A private bank opens in the kingdom, which has instituted fractional reserve lending. One enterprising village (Village A) borrows money to install a small water turbine and generator in the stream running through the village. The electricity generated by the turbine lights the village at night and enables the use of small power tools. Both boost the productivity of the village residents.

In effect, the money loaned by the bank has a multiplier effect: though the money created by the loan is removed from circulation when the village pays the loan off, the productivity gains enabled by the investment in the turbine/generator boost the production of goods and services in the village. There is a real-world gain in economic activity long after the loan is paid off.

The residents of Village B borrowed money to construct lavish homes for themselves. The construction briefly boosted employment and the purchase of building materials, but after the homes were completed, economic activity fell off; there were no gains in long-term productivity.

In terms of conventional bank underwriting and risk assessment, Village A's loan for the turbine/generator was riskier than the home loans. Village B's home loan was based on the borrower's ability to service the loan, i.e. make the monthly payments of principal and interest, and on the estimated value of the new home. The loan to Village A was deemed riskier, because who was responsible for making the monthly payment was diffused and therefore uncertain.

In terms of underwriting, the bank was blind to the key difference between Village A's *investment in assets that boosted long-term productivity* and Village B's *investment in consumption* (the lavish houses) that did nothing to boost productivity. The only criterion that mattered to the bank was the ability of the borrower to service the loan. The profound difference between investment in higher productivity and consumption didn't matter to the bank; as long as the borrowers made their payments and the bank earned a profit, the loans were of equal value to the bank, and indeed, to the entire banking system.

The bank was equally blind to the difference between a loan that *boosted the long-term well-being and prosperity of an entire community* and one that *boosted the consumption of one household.* To the banking sector, boosting the consumption of one household is the same as boosting the productivity of an entire community if both are creditworthy.

Profit-driven banking has no interest in the difference between the two, as its prime directive is to book as much short-term profit as possible. The long-term consequences have no impact on the banking sector's decision to lend; if the asset is presumed to hold its value and the borrower is deemed able to make the monthly payments, the loans are considered to be equally worthy.

This blindness to the profoundly significant differences between types of loans—between increasing productivity and unproductive consumption— highlights the perverse blindness and incentives of our current banking system.

A few of the Village B villagers found they could no longer pay their home loans, and they tried to sell their lavish homes to pay off the debt. But the lavish homes had no functional value beyond providing shelter, something a much cheaper home provided equally well - so nobody was willing to pay the high price asked by the villagers, and ownership of the homes reverted to the bank as the villagers defaulted.

The bank was only able to recover half of each loan when it sold the houses, and the losses pushed the bank into insolvency. The villagers who squandered the borrowed money on unproductive lavish homes were poorer than they were before they borrowed the money, and the village was also poorer as a result. Those who lost their cash deposits in the bank when the bank closed its doors were also poorer.

This example shows how leverage—loaning $20 into existence from $1 in cash—appears magical when the money is wisely invested in boosting long-term productivity. But when it is mal-invested in consumption or speculative assets, the losses cascade through the entire system: everyone becomes poorer when the borrowed money disappears from circulation.

The key point here is the peculiar ability of money created in excess to make people poorer: when the State or central bank issued money in excess, the resulting loss of purchasing power effectively reduces everyone's income. When the new money created by private bank lending is squandered, everyone—even those who did not borrow the money—become poorer as the costs of the mal-investment and losses spread beyond the bank and the borrowers.

Though it seems obvious that poverty is not having enough money, we now understand that it isn't quite as simple as that; borrowing too much money into existence makes everyone poorer.

The ideal money supply is one that is inextricably linked to the real-world expansion of goods and services and the widespread improvement of productivity. Unfortunately, money created by central banks and fractional reserve lending from private banks is not connected to the real-world expansion of goods and services or the long-term improvement of productivity at all. Instead, in the current system, money is created to serve the interests of the few and to generate short-term profits for banks.

The ideal banking system would create new money only to boost long-term productivity, not to fund unproductive consumption, and it would recognize the difference between boosting the productivity of an entire community and enabling the profligate consumption of a single household.

As we have seen, such a system must be decentralized and limited to creating money only in conjunction with the expansion of goods and services.

Money Issued by the Central Bank Benefits the Privileged

Let's imagine that we have a $1 billion line of credit with our central bank at an interest rate of 0.25%--one-quarter of 1%. We don't need to post any collateral, and the central bank has given us whispered assurances that should we lose the money in risky gambles, the losses will be made good by the taxpayers. This is called *moral hazard*: the risks have been disconnected from the consequences.

- If we make a profit with the borrowed money, it's ours to keep. If we lose the borrowed money, the taxpayers will foot the bill. It's difficult to imagine a better deal: near-zero interest rate, no collateral, and no risk of having to suffer the consequences of losing the borrowed money.
- But our advantages are even better than this already astonishing deal: with the magic of *fractional reserve banking*, we get to create $19 billion of new money with our $1 billion of borrowed central bank money.
- Our options for making low-risk profits are nearly limitless. Anything we earn beyond the annual interest of $2.5 million is ours to keep. We could invest the $1 billion in Treasury bonds yielding 2%. That would yield us an annual gain of $17.5 million for doing absolutely nothing beyond clicking a few keys to buy $1 billion Treasury bonds.
- If we are willing to take on higher risk, we could buy stocks that pay dividends of 3% or more annually. If the stocks rise in value, then we'd also earn capital gains. An annual gain of $30 million or more is easily possible in the relatively low-risk investment.
- If we wanted even higher yields, we could seek out bonds in other countries that are paying 6%. If those currencies are strengthening versus the U.S. dollar, then this foreign-exchange gain could boost our total gain to 10% annually—a cool $100 million, out of which we only have to pay the central bank a modest $2.5 million in interest.
- Or we could set up a bank that issues auto loans and credit cards with the $1 billion. Thanks to fractional reserve lending, our $1 billion in cash (never mind it was borrowed from the central bank—to the rest of the world, it's cash) can leverage $19 billion in high-interest consumer loans. If the average interest paid on our loan portfolio is 10%, we are earning $1.9 billion in gross revenues. If operating the bank costs $900 million, we net a cool $1 billion annually from the $1 billion line of credit: 100% annual return.

This is precisely how our current banking system works, and it illustrates how central banks enable private banks to accrue vast profits. Those closest to the central bank money-spigot are given an opportunity to leverage up *astounding* profits.

In theory, central banks claim the noble task of providing credit to the private banking sector to facilitate increased production of goods and services, but in reality central banks benefit the few with access to their credit - at the expense of the many. The few can generate immense profits without producing any goods and services whatsoever.

Imagine if we each had a relatively tiny $1 million line of credit at 0.25% interest from a central bank that we could use to issue loans of $19 million. Let's say we issued $19 million in home loans with an annual interest rate of 4%. The gross revenue (before expenses) of our leveraged $1 million is $760,000 annually. Since the accounting of the $19 million in loans is highly automated, our expenses are modest. Let's assume we net $600,000 per year after annual expenses of $160,000. Recall that the interest due on the $1 million line of credit is a paltry $2,500 annually.

Current median income for workers in the U.S. is around $30,000 annually. Thus a modest $1 million line of credit at .25% interest from the central bank enables us to net 20 years of a typical worker's earnings *every single year*.

But sadly, central banks don't offer this largesse to individuals or communities. These profoundly profitable privileges are available only to private banks.

I hope you now understand that the current system of issuing money and credit *intrinsically benefits the privileged few at the expense of the many*. This vast privilege and the equally vast inequality that *is the only possible output of the system* cannot be reformed away; it is intrinsic to centrally issued money and private banking.

The problem isn't *fiat money* (currency that isn't backed by scarce commodities) – rather, the problem is centrally issued money that is distributed to the few at the expense of the many. This centrally created money is not issued to facilitate the production of goods and services, but simply to serve the privileged.

Centrally issued money centralizes wealth and thus necessarily generates systemic inequality. This is equally true of all centrally issued currencies. The inequity that is intrinsic to this system is politically and financially destabilizing.

Given the intrinsic inequality of central banking and the perverse incentives of profit-driven fractional reserve banking, the ideal banking system must be decentralized such that *new money is issued directly to those generating new goods and services at the source of production.*

Those Who Create Money Can Buy the World (Assets and Power)

The power to issue money and credit makes financial capital the Master Resource in the world, because the newly-issued money can buy everything else: real-world assets such as land, oil and gold, and all forms of political power.

By granting central and private banks the power to create money via the digital printing press and fractional reserve lending, we have granted the banks and their cronies the power to buy everything else in the world with their newly issued money. No one earning money can possibly outbid those who can either create money or borrow essentially unlimited sums of money at near-zero rates of interest!

As a result, wealth-generating assets and political power inevitably end up in the hands of those with access to newly issued money/credit. Recent studies have found that a handful of wealthy people contribute most of the money that controls our political system. This outcome is not a surprise when we remember that *it is the only possible outcome of the current system for creating money and credit.* There is no other possible output other than wealth and political power being concentrated in the hands of those with the power to create money.

Restricting the power to create money to a handful of those at the top of the financial pyramid institutionalizes wealth inequality. *There is no other possible output from this system of creating money other than permanent wealth inequality.* Furthermore, this makes *central and private bank control of creating money intrinsically and inescapably immoral.*

As noted earlier, those benefiting from this vast centralized power must mask its intrinsic immorality by insisting money is apolitical and amoral—that is, it has neither political or moral characteristics.

If there is anything that I hope I have demonstrated, it is that the process of creating money is *ontologically* (i.e. inherently and always) political. The only moral process for creating money is one where *new money is issued directly to those generating new goods and services at the source of production.*

Centralized Money Is the Source of Inequality

None of the existing money systems—using gold and silver as money, printing paper money, central bank-issued credit money, or digital currencies—address the root causes of poverty. Money is commonly considered to be apolitical and amoral, meaning it has no political or moral bias. But as shown above, *money is always and everywhere intrinsically political* and thus has a moral component that is integral to its political nature.

The only way a system of creating and distributing money can claim to be moral is if it explicitly addresses the root cause of poverty (which as we've seen is the lack of paid work). Since none of the conventional systems of money creation and distribution—State issuance of paper money, central bank credit money or gold-backed currency—address the origins of poverty, *each is explicitly immoral.*

The only way a system of money creation can directly address poverty is to bypass the bottleneck of State/central bank political influence by distributing money directly to the public. The only way such a decentralized system can distribute money with sustainably moral incentives is *if labor itself creates money.*

In other words, the only moral mechanism for creating money is to take money issuance away from the central State and bank and make the creation of money the immediate consequence of productive labor.

How can productive labor create money? The answer is simple: money could be created digitally upon confirmation that productive work was performed and goods or services were created.

Digital currencies have demonstrated that the technology already exists to create money in a non-State, decentralized manner. What is needed is a mechanism that ties the creation of money to the one thing people mired in poverty have in abundance: their time and labor.

This mechanism could be realized in open-source software that would be accessible to any networked digital device. In low-income areas, this device is typically a low-cost mobile phone.

To operate in a sustainable fashion, this software would have to formalize a set of incentives in the rules that govern the authentication of digital payments for productive labor

The concept of a labor-based system of money creation and distribution is counter-intuitive to the conventional assumptions about money (i.e. that it must be issued by centralized authorities, that sound money is apolitical and amoral, and so on). That these ideological beliefs pass for truth is certainly convenient for the elites that control the majority of the wealth, money creation and productive assets. In the elite's carefully choreographed universe, poverty has essentially nothing to do with how money is created and distributed, even though in reality poverty is the direct consequence of being left out of the system of money creation and distribution.

The belief that money is apolitical and amoral is particularly convenient to ruling elites, as it masks the inherently political nature of money creation and distribution. The fact that every conventional money system coincides with entrenched poverty is attributed not to the money system but to external factors such as the paucity of natural resources, an oppressive social system, lack of educational opportunities and so on rather than to the construct of the money system itself.

To claim that the money system is somehow independent of the political-economic system it supports is to be willfully blind to the *political and moral ontology of money*.

I cannot imagine a more perfect protection for the privileged elites than the belief that money is disconnected from the mechanisms that govern the concentration of wealth and power. The ideal defense against charges that the mechanisms of exploitation are immoral is for the elites to deny that the mechanisms have a moral component. In essence, the argument that money is apolitical and amoral is equivalent to the elites saying: "We are wealthy and powerful not because the system is designed to enrich us and concentrate power in our hands, but because we are lucky, talented and/or divinely deserving."

Given the *ontological immorality of centrally controlled money*, the only way to wrest control from vested interests (who by their very existence create inequality) is to give the power to create and distribute money to a decentralized system that *distributes the money not by favoritism to the few but to the productive labor of the many*.

I describe this mechanism in my book *A Radically Beneficial World*. In essence, what I propose is that *money be created and distributed at the bottom of the pyramid for purposeful work that serves the community* rather than at the top of the pyramid of privilege.

Credit, Privilege, the State, Cartels and Monopolies

The State plays an essential role in enforcing the rigged games of monopolies and cartels, for the reason delineated by socio-historian Immanuel Wallerstein: ultimately, the State depends on high profits for its own tax revenues, and so enforcing monopolies and cartels is in the State's best interests.

The problem with monopolies and cartels is that they can raise the price of goods and services without increasing the quality or supply of goods and services. In effect, they extract a tax on consumers that flows as *rent* (hence the term *rentier class*) to the owners of the cartel/monopoly and then on to the State via taxes.

The State is of course the ultimate monopoly, as it has the sole power to use force to collect taxes and to create currency (money). It also has the power to raise revenues administratively, by understating inflation, increasing fees, raising tuition at State universities, and so on.

Economic Stagnation

Economies dominated by rentier cartels, monopolies and the State are stagnant economies, as the unproductive rents collected diminish the pool of private capital available for productive investment. With guaranteed profits and tax revenues, there are few incentives to increase efficiency or productivity. The State's enforcement of favored cartels and guilds (notaries in France, public labor unions in the U.S.) bleeds off capital and stifles any innovation that threatens the State, cartels or guilds.

Since innovation and capital in all its forms are essential to increasing productivity, productivity in these protected economies stagnates, which means that profits and wages also stagnate for the unprivileged. The privileged few benefit at the expense of the economy's resilience. Stagnant economies dominated by self-serving elites/ guilds thus become increasingly brittle and prone to collapse.

Another source of crippling stagnation is the reliance on unproductive debt to fuel consumption and speculation. The difference between productive and unproductive debt is easily illustrated by the following examples.

Let's say a company borrows $10 million to buy back its own shares, effectively boosting the per-share market price of the company's stock. Does the higher stock price reflect an increase in revenues, profits or productivity?

No; the company is not producing any more goods and services. The real output in the real economy is unchanged. All that's changed is that the company's officers can now issue themselves enormous stock-option bonuses while the costs of servicing the $10 million in new debt are borne by the company.

Let's say the State borrows $10 million to build a bridge to a lightly populated island. The tolls collected by users of the new bridge could support a $100,000 loan. Since the residents have other means of transport, the productive/functional value of the bridge is at best $100,000. The other $9.9 million certainly boosted consumption of materials and created short-lived jobs, but the opportunity cost of this unproductive investment is significant: what else that would have been far more productive over the long-term could have been done with that $10 million?

When the State can borrow essentially unlimited sums, there is no need to calculate the opportunity costs and no incentive to use the borrowed money prudently and productively.

We can understand this intuitively: if we were presented with a credit card with no limit and the payments were made by others, why would we spend the money carefully?

To fully understand the incentives behind the unprecedented global increase in unproductive debt, we have to compare the profits earned from producing goods and services (which are declining due to global overcapacity, technology and competition), against the enormous profits that can be earned from speculating with leveraged debt.

The issuance of debt by banks is in itself phenomenally profitable, as we have seen. The tools of *financialization* (leverage, derivatives and securitization of debt) enable banks to reap profits on long-term loans and mortgages upfront and sell the securitized debt (and derivatives based on the underlying debt) to investors.

The structural decline in profits earned from producing goods and services has perversely incentivized the drive for profits earned from debt and speculation in financial markets. But as we saw with the above examples, this vast expansion of debt results not in increased production of goods/services, but instead in speculation that destabilizes the economy. After all, why risk capital in real-world innovation when the big profits are being made by debt-fueled speculation?

Unproductive debt is a short-term work-around for an economy that no longer profits from producing goods and services, but the cost in stability and productivity are staggering. Economies that rely on ever-rising debt to fund consumption and speculation generate outsized profits for the few at the expense of the many. In other words, the primary long-term output of these economies is widespread poverty.

The Dead-End of Privileged Finance: Financialization

As production reaches overcapacity and markets become saturated, profits from producing goods and services decline. The final remaining source of oversized profits is *financialization*, which is the process of transforming low-risk, low-profit debt into high-risk, high-profit speculation that enriches the financial sector and the State at the expense of other sectors of the economy.

Financialization does this by introducing perverse incentives that distort and weaken the economy. The huge profits to be reaped from financializing debt leads households and enterprises alike to over-invest in highly risky speculation at the expense of productive investments.

When the profits made by leveraging debt-based speculation far exceeds the income from creating products and services, the economy is hollowed out, since the perverse incentives of financialization drive the decisions and strategies of businesses and households.

- Rather than invest in risky research and development projects, corporations borrow money to buy back their own stocks, boosting capital gains and management bonuses.
- Private equity borrows money to buy existing companies, because strip-mining their assets is far more profitable than risking capital in start-up ventures with high failure rates.
- Financialization effectively drains safe income from households and forces savers onto the tilted game board of risky speculation—a game the average wage-earner is unlikely to win, especially when critical information about risk is kept secret by the financial heavyweights who originate the financial instruments in play. As an example, home mortgages once operated as a financial utility: banks issued low-risk, low-yield mortgages and held the loans to maturation. Financialization transformed this low-risk investment into a high-risk speculation by bundling mortgages into pools that were then divided into tranches and sold as low-risk securities.

Financialization claims to increase profits at near-zero risk, but this is an illusion: risk and return are inextricably linked. Enormous profits can only arise from enormous risks, and the process of financialization purposely masks those risks to offload risky securities onto unwary investors.

This *asymmetry of information* available to the seller vs. the buyer shifts risk to those least prepared to deal with it prudently: unwary buyers of risky assets. When only the sellers know the risks, buyers cannot possibly make informed, prudent decisions. This creates a perverse incentive for sellers to hide risk and leads buyers to over-invest in highly risky assets—a recipe for catastrophic financial losses.

My personal definition of financialization is:

Financialization is the mass commodification of debt and debt-based financial instruments collaterized by previously low-risk assets; a pyramiding of risk and speculative gains that requires a massive expansion of credit and leverage.

1. The first key to financialization is that the collateral—corporate assets and cash flow, commercial real estate, homes, etc.—is commoditized, i.e. turned into financial instruments that can be freely traded in the global market. A leveraged mountain of debt is erected on the collateral, so that each $1 of collateral can support multiple dollars of debt, which can then support debt-based derivatives.

    In a financialized system, credit and leverage both expand mightily, but the collateral supporting this expanding mountain of debt and leverage remains unchanged. The risk in this game is obvious: if $2 of collateral is supporting $20 of debt, a decline of $1 in the value of the collateral doubles the leverage in the system. A loss of the $2 of collateral doesn't trigger a write-down of $2 in losses—in a financialized system, it triggers $20 in losses that then topple other financial dominoes as the losses cause a revaluation of collateral and a freezing of credit.

2. The second key to financialization is *information asymmetry*, where the elites know more information about the risks than the regulators and investors, who thus have a weakened grasp of the risks building up along with their debt and leverage.

The systemic consequence of financialization is the renunciation of productive investment for the oversized profits of unproductive speculation. *When leverage and information asymmetry replace innovation and productive investment as the source of wealth creation, the productive sectors of the economy wither, and the least productive sector—finance—attracts the most talent and capital.* As a result, the productive economy is starved of talent and capital, and productivity stagnates. Since increasing productivity is the driver of widespread gains in capital and wealth, the economy becomes poorer as more and more capital and income is siphoned off by speculators with access to cheap credit.

In effect, financialization is the plundering of the productive economy by the parasitic, predatory financial sector. This process is a dead-end, because once the available collateral has been leveraged, there is nothing left to financialize, and the top-heavy financial sector (now the most profitable sector of the economy) implodes, taking the rest of the hollowed out economy with it.

This process of financialization is necessarily impoverishing, since productive assets are stripped of value and the remaining wealth is concentrated in the hands of the elite speculators with access to central bank credit.

Financialization is an insidious pathology. The asset bubbles it inflates appear at first to be 'tides that raise all ships'; during the credit-based speculative expansion, prosperity seems to be increasing everywhere for all participants. But when the bubble pops, as all bubbles eventually do, the financiers protected from losses by the State—moral hazard writ large—retain all their profits skimmed in the expansion, while the losses are socialized, i.e. transferred to taxpayers.

This enormous transfer of wealth impoverishes the many to the benefit of the few. Even more perverse is the erosion of productive investment, as this starves the economy of the engine of widespread prosperity: productivity.

Financialization thus impoverishes everyone but those protected from losses by the State and central bank, and it impoverishes the economy by diverting capital and talent away from productivity-increasing investments to unproductive debt and speculation.

The perverse incentives reinforced by financialization are a one-way street to impoverishment for all but the few at the top of the pyramid of power. Once productivity stagnates, a complete collapse of credit and leverage is the only possible end-game of financialization.

The Dependence of "Good" Investment on "Bad" Financialization

The outsized gains reaped by leveraged financialization and the central bank's subsequent reduction of interest rates to near-zero to protect the financial sector from the consequences of speculative excess have perversely left investments we consider "good" (such as pension funds) completely dependent on "bad" speculation that is systemically destabilizing. This has created two sources of systemic risk:

1. Stripped of any yield in safe investments by central bank policies designed to rescue the "bad" banks, "good" pension and retirement funds have no alternative but to accept the tremendous risks intrinsic to speculative gambles.
2. This dynamic insures "good" institutional investors will eventually suffer the same catastrophic losses that sank the "bad" banks, forcing the state to rescue the "good" investors. Since the deadwood of failed bets is never cleared, systemic risk rises with every state bailout.

Why do "good" investors chase high yields and accept the equally high risks? Because pension funds and insurers must earn relatively high returns to pay their promised pensions and payouts. The managers of these funds (along with individuals and enterprises managing 401K and other retirement funds) have no choice but to shoulder high risks to get high yields, lest the funds go broke or fail to pay the promised payouts.

Not only has this placed "good" investments at the mercy of the most destabilizing dynamics in the financial world, but this dependence has also greatly increased the pressure on the State to rescue the very players that would be eliminated from the system when the credit bubble collapses.

Perversely, the dependence of retirement accounts and State revenues on "bad" speculation increases the systemic risk of a collapse that cannot be fixed with the usual central bank tricks of lowering interest rates and increasing credit.

I call this dynamic of perversely increasing systemic risk *The Yellowstone Analogy*, as it closely parallels the risks and consequences that arise when all forest fires are immediately suppressed: eventually, the deadwood that would naturally have been cleared in limited burns piles so high that when the forest does catch fire in a random lightning strike, the resulting conflagration cannot be controlled, and the entire forest burns to the ground.

In our financial analogy, speculative excesses of credit and leverage produce the deadwood of loans that cannot be paid, and rising debt teetering on phantom collateral. In capitalism, as in Nature, the limited fires of credit contraction and bankruptcy routinely clear the financial forest of this deadwood. As in a forest, the ashes of speculative excess provide the foundation for the next cycle of productive growth.

But as soon as "good" investment is at risk if the speculative excesses are reduced to ashes, no cleansing fire can be allowed, and the financial deadwood of bad debt and phantom collateral continues to expand.

This highly flammable bramble of leverage, risk and debt will eventually be ignited by some financial equivalent of a lightning strike, and the resulting conflagration will burn down the entire global financial system—not just the "bad" speculators but the "good" investments that became dependent on risky financialization for their high returns.

What is particularly interesting in this dynamic is how every player *has no choice but to participate in a system that is guaranteed to Implode.*

- The banks and financiers have no choice but to pursue financialization as the only means left to earn outsized profits;
- The pension funds have no choice but to participate in this to get the high yields they need to function; and
- The State and central banks have no choice but to rescue the increasingly vulnerable system every time it threatens to collapse.

Perversely, every rescue increases the system's vulnerability and ensures the next even bigger crisis and ever more extreme rescue. *This self-reinforcing cycle has no possible outcome other than collapse.*

A Systemic Source of Privilege: Externalizing Costs

When enterprises offload production costs onto the system at large, economists refer to this as *externalizing costs*.

For example, both pollution and the future costs of healthcare for workers whose health has been damaged by the pollution are costs that have been shifted to both the *Biosphere Commons* (of air, sea, fresh water, soil) and to the public in order to maximize private profits.

In the case of environmental damage caused by privately owned production, the profits being reaped are in effect illusory; because if the costs of cleaning up the damage and the resulting healthcare burdens caused by pollution deducted from the claimed profit, the profit would turn into a loss.

In other words, a significant percentage of the private profits being reaped globally are not actual profits—they are the result of production costs being passed onto others while the gains are kept for the owners.

Author John Michael Greer characterizes the current world-system as *"an arrangement set up to allow a privileged minority to externalize nearly all their costs onto the rest of society while pocketing as much as possible of the benefits themselves."*

The resulting concentration of profits into a few hands and the externalization of costs to everyone else results in rising wealth and income inequality. Thus what Thomas Piketty and others have identified as the primary source of wealth inequality—capital expanding at a higher rate than the overall economy expands—is more properly understood as *production costs being externalized by capital.* This externalization of costs boosts profits for those who own the capital by distributing these expenses to others.

Thus the stated profits are not honest profits; they are simply the gains reaped by passing production costs (current and future) on to everyone else.

Those most adept at externalizing costs have purchased enforcement of their privileges from the State. Since the gains are concentrated and the costs diffused, vested interests will do everything possible to protect their right to keep externalizing their costs. Otherwise, as Greer has pointed out, the costs they would have to absorb would come right out of their 'profits', while the benefits of reducing costs being distributed to the public would be spread over the entire populace. As Mancur Olson observed, incentives guide economics. The few have very powerful incentives (i.e. immense private profits) to externalize costs while the benefits from resisting the externalization are so diffused that the general public has little incentive to do so.

This externalization of production costs is driven by the incentives to book ever-larger profits and by the systemic rise in structural costs. Immanuel Wallerstein identified four such structural drivers:

1. Urbanization of the global populace (wages and costs are higher in urban zones)
2. The external costs of industrialization (mitigating pollution, etc.)

3. The rising costs of labor overhead (pensions, healthcare, disability insurance, etc.)
4. Rising demands on the State for more social spending on education, healthcare, retirees, etc.

As these systemic increases squeeze private profits and wages, the State faces a commensurate decline in its revenues. Who will pay these externalized costs? If the owners of capital are forced to pay, profits plummet. The only other way to reduce production costs is replace human labor with software and robotics, which further reduces wages. If wages and profits are declining, the State's revenues drop as well.

Once these externalized costs are properly accounted for, all the illusory profits (and State revenues derived from those illusory profits) vanish. Indeed, a recent study by the environmental consultancy Trucost on behalf of The Economics of Ecosystems and Biodiversity (TEEB) found that none of the world's top industries would be profitable if they paid for the natural capital they consume or use.

The State's role in the externalization of production costs is not a flaw that can be reformed away; it is *an intrinsic feature of the current mode of production* that is dominated by the collusion of private capital and the State. The State and its Elites depend on high private profits for their own revenues/wealth, and placing the future costs of today's production on the producers would reduce or eliminate those profits.

The concentrations of wealth that influence the State to protect their privilege to externalize costs are also intrinsic *features of* the current mode of production. This feedback loop—capital expands by limiting competition and externalizing costs courtesy of the State, which depends on the taxes and wages paid by profitable capital for its own revenues—cannot be broken lest the system implode.

It is important to understand that inequality arises not just from blatant exploitation or lack of resources. The current mode of production outputs inequality by enabling the privileged few to distribute costs to the system at large and siphon off the resulting profits as private gains—some of which are shared with the State in return for the privileges of limited competition and externalizing costs.

Once competition is limited, entrepreneurs are pushed into marginal markets and everyone else either works for the State or vested interests. Since building capital is perhaps the single most important step in reducing inequality and poverty, any system that makes it difficult for the poor to acquire productive capital *necessarily generates rising inequality and poverty*.

Shifting production costs (present and future) to the public also generates poverty, as income that could have been invested in productive uses is drained off to pay the externalized costs (air pollution, future healthcare costs, drained aquifers, poisoned water and soil, etc.) that were dumped by private capital on the public.

The system is not difficult to understand: limiting competition and externalizing costs benefit the few at the expense of the many. Thus limiting competition and externalizing costs are *the engines of inequality and poverty*.

The system that externalizes costs has every incentive to do so, as *any policy that reduced the engines of inequality would come straight out of private profits and State coffers*. The notion that vested interests and the State will happily fall on their financial swords to better the lives of the many runs counter to the incentives to maximize individual gain that dominate the current mode of production.

In other words, the system doesn't have to set a conscious goal of generating poverty in order to actually generate poverty—poverty is the unavoidable result of maximizing private gain and protecting the privileged.

The powerlessness of those forced to pay the externalized costs and toil in neofeudal servitude to the State and vested interests is also a necessary result of the current system. Nobody would consciously choose to poison the air their family is breathing to increase the profits of a handful of privileged elites. In the current system, the many have no choice; rising wealth for the few, powerlessness and poverty for the many are the only possible outputs.

The only way to ensure the many have a say over the Biosphere Commons is to take the decision-making away from the privileged and return it to the communities that must live with the consequences of production and consumption.

Chapter Five - The Nature of Political Privilege

The Destabilizing Co-Dependence of the State and Finance

In our taxonomy of privilege, we identified four related forms of political privilege:

1. Leveraging the power of the State to enforce private privileges
2. Patronage: obtaining privileges by serving political elites
3. Politically protected membership (guilds, unions, etc.)
4. Bureaucratic privilege: being rewarded for process rather than outcome

As I explained in my book *Resistance, Revolution, Liberation, the State has only one ontological imperative: expansion*. The government has no mechanisms for contraction; it only has mechanisms for expanding its reach and power.

I also described *the pathology of concentrated power*. The State concentrates power, which then attracts those seeking to leverage that power to their own private advantage.

If a cartel set out to control the economies of 1,000 different cities, the process would be time-consuming, costly and fraught with complexity. But once a central State controls the economies of the 1,000 cities, the cartel can then influence the central State via lobbying and bribes (often masked as political contributions or speaking fees) for a tiny percentage of the cost of buying influence in 1,000 cities. Just as financial leverage enables the financial elite to buy productive assets using low-cost credit and very little cash, the relatively low cost of political leverage within the central State enables the privileged few to control the machinery of governance for a thin slice of their wealth/income.

For example, a cartel might spend $10 million on lobbying and campaign contributions in exchange for tax breaks and subsidies worth $100 million. And since the cartel can borrow immense sums at rates unavailable to the unprivileged, the cartel can even buy political influence without spending any of its own cash! Meanwhile, the unprivileged cannot borrow such sums at low cost, so are effectively powerless in the pay-to-play political arena.

Concentrating power in the State enables private capital to concentrate its own power in a self-reinforcing cycle of increasing wealth and power: buying influence over the State suppresses competition which increases the profits of private capital that then funds additional influence over the State, and so on.

In the previous chapter on financial privilege, I explained how the State comes to depend on financialization for its tax revenues and how the neofeudal concentration of private wealth enables the financially privileged to buy State protection of cartels and monopolies that suppress competition and innovation that then cripple productivity. This establishes an insidiously perverse cycle in which the State cannot afford to limit the financialization that is hollowing out the economy and widening inequality.

The resulting stagnation favors the privileged, because the State protects its own privileged classes and the rigged games of financiers from the ravages of risk that are shoved onto the unprivileged. But this protection of State-private privilege is not sustainable. As inequality soars, the social and political orders are destabilized. As the economy stagnates, the unprivileged are no longer able to support their heavy debt loads, and defaults destroy the profits of financialization.

Just as the State has no mechanism for contraction, financialization has no mechanism for ending its dependence on the expansion of debt and leverage. Once debt ceases to expand, the system implodes.

This became evident to all in 2008, when the extremely modest deleveraging/reduction in debt resulting from subprime mortgages defaults nearly collapsed the entire global financial system.

The concentration of financial and political power in the State and the privileged financial elites inevitably creates *a self-reinforcing cycle of fragility, instability and collapse.*

As the economy becomes dependent on finance for its profits, its capacity to produce goods and services weakens from under-investment, State over-regulation/taxation, and the parasitic rigged games of privilege.

Educated elites learn to avoid risk by entering protected fiefdoms of the State and the financial sector, while the unprivileged seek the safety of State welfare. The economy loses its appetite for risk, which is the essential dynamic in boosting productivity: risk and return are inextricably linked, and once risk is avoided then stagnation and decline inevitably follow.

As the State expands on the back of financialization, it becomes so dominant that only those buying its favors can survive. This suppresses innovation, competition and risk-taking, hollowing out the private sector that funds the State's tax revenues.

Yet as the non-financial economy weakens and the privileged class siphon off most of the economy's gains, the State becomes increasingly dependent on borrowing money to fund its ballooning expenditures. This dependence on debt makes the State dependent on additional financialization, which further weakens the economy, which then drives the State to borrow more, and so on, until the entire State-finance mode of production collapses under the weight of soaring debt and stagnating productivity.

In effect, the State and finance are dependent on each other for their survival, but this co-dependence weakens the economy and widens the wealth/income gap between the protected privileged and the unprotected unprivileged. As this gap widens, resentment between the haves and the have-nots increases and social instability rises accordingly.

The State responds to this rising instability with two strategies: *political repression* and *more State welfare.* But both responses suppress the very elements of the economy and society that are needed to restore vitality and boost productivity, and as a result, the State's heavy-handed defense of its own privileges increases the fragility of the entire mode of production.

This feedback loop of increasing dependence on financialization, debt and repression of dissent leads inevitably to the collapse of the financial sector and, ultimately, the State itself.

Expansion of the State's Privileged Classes

As the State expands on the back of financialization, its protected class of employees and cronies also expands, to the point where it becomes powerful enough to protect and even further expand its own privileges. For example, as explained earlier, public-sector unions and the civil service extract pay and benefits far in excess of what the unprivileged private-sector workers receive for performing the same work.

- Just as the financial elite use the State's power to protect their privileges, the State's own employees and entrenched interests use the State's power to protect their own private privileges.
- Just as the expansion of privileged financial elites and the State widens inequality and increases systemic fragility, the expansion of the State's privileged classes weakens the system in self-reinforcing feedbacks.

Since the State's protected classes reward themselves for seniority and following process rather than for producing successful outcomes, they have essentially no skin in the game: as the economy weakens, the State raises taxes and/or borrows more money to fund their salaries and benefits.

As the State's share of the stagnating economy expands, profits and savings that could have been invested in productive assets are siphoned off to fund the State's dependents and bureaucracies. This creates a self-reinforcing feedback loop as higher taxes and State debt further weaken the economy, forcing the State to borrow more money and raise taxes, and so on until the system collapses under the weight of the State and its armies of dependents.

Democracy Dies When Newly Created Money Buys Political Power

The dominance of finance and the State has another consequence: the undermining and destruction of democracy.

In our current mode of production, those with the power to create money and credit have essentially unlimited sums with which to buy political power. As a direct result of this power to create money and credit, the political system is reduced to a continual auction of favors to the highest bidder. Those who can create money or credit in unlimited sums can always outbid anyone whose wealth is earned or limited to real-world assets. No sultan with mere oil or gold can possibly outbid those with the power to create unlimited money and credit at near-zero interest.

Concentrating the power to create money and credit in the hands of the few is fatal to democracy. No amount of reform can protect democracy from this financial toxin. Rather than being apolitical, the power to create and distribute currency and credit is inherently political, as the power to create money and credit buys not just assets but political power. A centralized money creation system that kills democracy by its very nature is *intrinsically immoral to its very core*.

The only way to safeguard democracy is to democratize the creation and distribution of money and credit so that *new money is only issued directly to those creating goods and services with their labor*.

I have already described such a system in my book *A Radically Beneficial World*.

Why Nations Fail: Enforced Stability of Privileged Vested Interests

Mancur Olson, Daron Acemoglu, James A. Robinson and others have studied why some economies fail to deliver widespread prosperity. The core dynamic can be summarized as the *enforced stability of vested interests*.

Here is how the dynamic works. Vested interests seek to maintain scarcity and set prices to ensure high wages and profits. Since the State's own revenues are derived from profits and wages, the State protects the scarcity and profits of vested interests to protect its own revenue and stability.

Since competition disrupts the high profits and wages of cartels and guilds, the State must limit competition to protect the stability of vested interests. The State thus enforces artificial scarcity (of goods, services, capital, etc.) and limits competition to the margins of the economy.

In other words, the system benefits the few at the expense of the many.

But as Olson observed, economies dominated by the enforced stability of vested interests become increasingly inefficient, as the incentives to increase productivity (and thus wealth) have been eliminated. Why take risks to increase productivity when profits and wages of the privileged are guaranteed? The highest return is gained by lobbying State Elites to protect the monopolies from the volatility and instability of competition.

As Nassim Taleb has shown in his work, a constant flux of dissent, volatility and instability is a critical requirement of sustainably stable systems. *Any system that limits dissent, volatility and instability in effect guarantees its eventual destabilization and collapse*.

With these requirements are absent, productivity and competition stagnate. Since wealth results from increasing productivity, economies dominated by the enforced stability of vested interests inevitably experience increasing wealth inequality and poverty.

This systemic protection of vested interests is institutionalized by the state, with a wide spectrum of enforcement methods. Some societies use quasi-official corruption; others eschew petty corruption but informally auction political favors to the highest bidder under the guise of pay-to-play political campaign contributions Regardless of the specific methods used to protect the privileges of vested interests, the net result is the same: *enforced stability of vested interests*.

Every system that enforces the stability of increasingly inefficient, predatory and parasitic vested interests dooms itself to stagnation and collapse. Every such system generates endemic poverty as a result of its forced stability - and catastrophic poverty when it collapses.

The State Enforces Moral Hazard, the Foundation of Privilege

The *ontological imperative* of the State is to expand its control. The State has only one mode of existence: expansion. It has no internal mechanisms for contraction. From the State's point of view, everything outside its control poses a potential risk, and the only way to lower risk is to control everything that can be controlled.

State control institutionalizes moral hazard, which is *the separation of risk from gain*. The key characteristic of moral hazard can be stated very simply:

People who are exposed to risk and consequence make very different choices than those who are not exposed to risk and consequence.

The potential for loss (i.e. risk) is an essential input in decision-making and the allocation of resources, capital and labor. If there is no risk of loss (i.e. negative consequence), participants can reap private gains at will, free-riding off the labor and capital of others.

When the State enables moral hazard, highly risky speculative bets can be placed with impunity by individuals seeking to maximize their private gains, because the State's taxpayers shoulder the risk of loss. In effect, all risk in the system is transferred to the State's citizens, as the State holds protected elites harmless from loss.

From the perspective of risk, the State's primary role is enforcing moral hazard, by separating the consequences of failure, waste, inefficiency and bad bets from those who make State policies.

The vast majority of those working in State agencies do not suffer any real consequences should the agencies fail to achieve their public purposes. State employees don't lose their jobs, benefits or pensions if the agency fails or they perform their duties poorly; they have no real *skin in the game*.

On the other end of the scale, those receiving State social welfare also have no skin in the game. Their State benefits are guaranteed regardless of their actions.

Moral hazard is thus fed from both ends: by those managing the State and those dependent on its cash transfers.

The essence of moral hazard is the transfer of risk to the unprotected taxpayers.

Moral hazard institutionalized by the State has numerous self-reinforcing consequences. Authors Franz Kafka and George Orwell addressed these consequences many years ago in their writings.

- A lawyer by training and practice, Kafka understood that the more powerful and entrenched the State bureaucracy, the greater the collateral damage rained on the innocent and the more extreme the perversions of justice. This is the direct result of centralization's inherent imposition of moral hazard and transfer of risk and loss to the unprotected.
- Orwell understood that the State's ontological imperative is expansion. Once the State has expanded beyond the control of the citizenry, it becomes the haven of those seeking to leverage its power to their own advantage. Protected behind the thick walls of the State, the few are free to plunder the many without consequence.

This is the primary result of the 2008 financial crisis and the emergence of "too big to fail, too big to jail" banks protected from the consequences of their reckless speculations by the State and its central bank. But this is also precisely how nations fail. Centralized power protects vested interests from consequence, at the expense of everyone below this apex of power.

We can now understand Wallerstein's characterization of the current mode of production: as *"a particular historical configuration of markets and State structures where private economic gain by almost any means is the paramount goal and measure of success."*

There are also no consequences to employees of the State if its bureaucracies fail to alleviate poverty. The lowest-cost method of dealing with poverty is to issue just enough 'bread and circuses' to keep the poor resigned and politically passive. This is what moral hazard incentivizes, and so this is the inevitable output of the system.

Any system that enforces moral hazard is intrinsically incapable of solving rising inequality, for *moral hazard creates systemic inequality*, where those freed from consequences and risks are also free to exploit those who are still exposed to consequences and risks.

This diversion of potentially productive capital to the most unproductive sectors impoverishes the entire economy by bleeding off the capital needed to boost productivity. Any system beset with moral hazard cannot possibly boost productivity or distribute the gains from rising productivity widely, as whatever gains are generated in the system are commandeered by those protected from risk and consequence. This is the perfection of *malinvestment of capital.*

That centralized States are characterized by corruption, favoritism, nepotism, "too big to fail," fraud, embezzlement, sweetheart deals, insider trading, free-riding, rackets, catastrophically unproductive investments, waste and endemic inefficiency is no mere accident. These are the inescapable fruits of moral hazard.

Once a participant (public or private) is protected from risk by the State, the incentives built into the system encourage predatory, parasitic exploitation of whatever resources are within reach. For the low-level bureaucrat, this might be restricted to exploiting whatever petty powers have been granted to him by the State; for financiers close to the money-spigots of the central bank, it might be skimming tens of billions of dollars annually.

The difference between the two is not in the mechanisms of moral hazard, but only in their access to plunder.

The State's Role as Enforcer of Privilege

Broadly speaking, the status quo protects the privileged from risk and accountability, and the State enforces those privileges. The State has exclusive rights to three tools of enforcement:

1. Police/military force,
2. The creation/distribution of currency, and
3. The pledging taxpayers' incomes, present and future, to borrow money on the State's behalf.

The ability of the State to impose regulations, imprison dissidents, funnel money to cronies, and borrow money to fund the State's privileged classes is unmatched. This monopoly on regulation, force, currency and sovereign debt enables the State to transfer risk and accountability from its protected classes onto the unprivileged, unprotected citizenry.

The State enforces a specific structure of power, opportunity, responsibility and risk (PORR) to protect the privileged. The State's tools enable both heavy-handed repression via outlawing threats to its protected classes, and erecting regulatory barriers that effectively eliminate competition and suppress innovation by raising the costs of compliance.

As with many manifestations of privilege, the State masks its protection of privilege behind public-relations claims of 'fairness' and 'transparency'. The State can claim to allow competition and dissent while actually suppressing both with legal and regulatory burdens.

Unfortunately for the protected privileged, *risk cannot be extinguished, it can only be transferred.* By transferring risk, accountability and costs to the class that has the fewest resources to mitigate crises and poor outcomes—the unprotected unprivileged—the State ensures risk will pile up in the most fragile sectors of the system. But once the risk crushes the unprotected, it topples the most fragile sectors, which then take down the rest of the economy until even the finances of the formerly invulnerable State collapse.

Four Privileged Classes

The State is actually comprised of four separate privileged classes, as follows (listed in decreasing order of power/control):

1. The class of *financial nobility* that leverages the power of the State to protect its private privileges via lobbying, campaign contributions, bribes and revolving doors between State regulatory agencies and plum positions in private companies.
2. The *patronage class* that secures privileges by serving the interests of political elites.
3. The class of *State employees* that receives pay and benefits far in excess of what unprotected private-sector workers get for doing the same work, and who cannot be fired even if the outcome of their work is poor and the economy is stagnating.
4. The class with *bureaucratic privileges* who are rewarded for process rather than outcome (i.e. their failure has no adverse consequence on their pay, benefits or security).

Note that the State's privileged classes include not just State employees but also private-sector contractors and financial elites.

Where We Are Now: The Inevitable Collapse of Debt-Funded, State-Enforced Privilege

As we have seen, in the initial stages of financialization and expansion of the State, it seems that protecting the privileged classes is cost-free. It is only later, as the self-reinforcing feedbacks weaken the entire mode of production, does it become apparent that the costs of protecting State and financial class privileges are unsustainable. In our current mode of production, the protected classes are so entrenched politically that it is impossible to dislodge their privileges – and it is at that point that the system is destined to collapse under its own unproductive weight.

Chapter Six - Narratives that Enforce Privilege

The Limits of the System's Two Narratives: The Market and the State

Those of us embedded in the current mode of production naturally assume this is *the only possible way of organizing human life*. The dominance of centralized markets and states was described by 20th century sociologist Max Weber, who proposed that these organizing principles would inevitably dominate every formal institution.

The problem is that each of these organizational ideas only functions within a narrow spectrum of utility and competence. Once applied to every institution and practice, the market and the State are both subject to the Peter Principle, i.e. *they rise to the highest level of their incompetence*.

Since alternative principles for organizing life have been either marginalized, outlawed, or neglected, participants keep applying these two dominant organizing principles, the Market and the State, to every problem, even when they are clearly *the wrong unit size* and their practices counterproductive.

In the current mode of production, there are only two solutions offered for any problem:

1. Create a market whose organizing principle is maximizing private profits, or
2. Give the State more power and wealth to address the problem.

That these two principles are incapable of solving problems outside their narrow areas of competence simply doesn't compute for most participants, who believe *these must be the solution because there are no other options*. This is obviously false; there are alternatives, but there is no intellectual, financial and political space for them in the current system. As Weber pointed out, this is not the result of human intent; it is the natural result of applying these two organizational principles to every aspect of human life. What isn't advertised is that the combination of these organizational principles is ideal for creating and enforcing privilege.

The Conceptual Poverty of Our Dominant Narratives

The profound intellectual poverty of these two purported solutions—the neoliberal ideology of making everything into a market organized to maximize private gain (also known as 'capitalism'), and the expansion of State power (aka 'socialism')—parallels the material and social poverty the current system generates.

The dominant narratives constructed around these two ideas—capitalism and socialism—both suffer from a mechanistic reduction of human life and the material world to the invisible hand of markets and the central-planning of the State.

The dominance of these principles of production and governance has effectively rewritten history to suggest that the market and the State are all we've ever had and all we'll ever have. The possibility that there are other principles for production and governance that are more productive, sustainable, fair and efficient is almost inconceivable.

Marx and Keynes believed that their economic systems would lead to the Heaven of equality and free time for everyone to have fun and gain fulfillment. Neither had much interest in exploring what human beings actually need for fulfillment, and this vast ignorance is reflected in the reductionist limits of their economic ideologies and the failure of these ideas to reverse rising inequality.

We now understand that the starting place for designing a system that outputs human fulfillment is the *social order's mode of production,* not mechanistic models of economics that assume humans are either saints or rational economic machines.

 If we step back from the dominant narratives, we are astonished by their reduction of complex systems to mechanistic models, as if measuring output, credit and consumption are all that's needed to organize a sustainable, humane order. Yet we continue to be reassured that whatever the invisible hand of maximizing private gain fails to do, the central State can do.

The problem with the idea that the State is the solution to all problems is that centralizing the issuance and distribution of money, and centralizing political power, inevitably centralizes private wealth and power, as those closest to the State money spigot gain private wealth which then buys political power.

It is clear that the market and the State are really just two aspects of one overall organizing principle: maximize private gain and power. The key mechanism for doing so is to gain control of *value creation*. Since value is created by scarcity and demand, the way to control value creation is to *enforce scarcity of what is in demand* (for example, the necessities of life), *limit the ability of others to address scarcity*, i.e. limit competition, and *limit the issuance of money and cheap credit to the select few*.

That these mechanisms *are immoral because their only possible output is rising inequality* is actively obfuscated by the current narratives. The market-State narratives are not just intellectually impoverished, they are morally impoverished. Few of the masses understand that the willful moral blindness of these narratives serves only the power of the few at the expense of the many.

Privilege Eliminates Feedback, Leading to Instability

The long-term stability of natural systems stems from the self-regulatory mechanisms of feedback.

Feedback can be positive (reinforcing the current trend) or negative (countering the current trend). In natural systems, extremes rarely endure, because opposing feedback generates counter-trends that moderate the extreme. Natural selection is a form of feedback, as organisms and systems experiment with a variety of adaptations to survive changing conditions. When feedback is suppressed, adaptation is suppressed as well. Then, when conditions change, the only possible result of suppressing feedback/adaptation is failure to adapt - i.e. systemic collapse.

The essence of the current world-system is that any feedback that threatens the power and wealth of those at the apex is suppressed. This includes democracy, which is a form of self-regulating feedback. Even the business cycle, which is the interplay of the negative and positive feedbacks of risk appetite and avoidance/credit expansion and contraction, is now viewed as a threat to the permanent expansion of credit needed to sustain the current world-system.

For the elites in our current world-system, feedback is viewed as a threat to their security. From their perspective, democracy is a force that, if left unchecked, threatens the wealth and control of those at the top of the power pyramid. And the social welfare programs so 'generously' permitted by the elites is not really compassion-in-action; it is merely the lowest cost method of dissipating social unrest arising from the extremes of wealth and income inequality.

So from a systems analysis perspective, the current mode of production protects itself from threats by suppressing feedback. But, seemingly unrecognized even by the elites, by suppressing feedback, the system has crippled the very mechanisms of dissent, innovation and self-regulation necessary for its long-term stability.

The only possible output of a system that suppresses feedback is self-reinforcing instability and collapse.

The Incentive Structure of the Current Mode of Production

Economics is often presented as a dizzying intellectual battleground of competing schools and equations. Within specific topics, this can certainly be true. But economics in the real world boils down to just plain incentives: *what incentives and disincentives are available to participants?* Incentives and the risks of loss or punishment guide our economic behaviors and choices.

A policy is designed to incentivize specific choices and behaviors to reach a desired goal. But humans (along with other organisms) are acutely sensitive to windfalls. We automatically seek opportunities where a very little work yields a highly desirable payoff. This cost-benefit analysis is a built-in survival mechanism, because calories (energy) were scarce in the world we inhabited as hunter-gatherers. Whatever opportunity reaps the biggest gain for the least risk and expenditure of energy always gets exploited first—the low hanging fruit gets picked first.

Our risk-return analysis is similarly acute. If the risk of disastrous consequences is high, we're cautious. If our risk can be shared among others, we become more adventurous. If the risk can be completely off-loaded onto others, then our appetite for risk soars, since the gains (if any) will be ours to keep while the consequences will fall on others.

This is the definition of *moral hazard*: the severing of risk from consequence.

Those bearing the risks will act quite differently than those who have offloaded costs and consequences to others.

If I enter a casino and have to use my own money, I make only small bets and leave when I've lost my limited cash. But if you give me a million dollar line of credit, and say that the casino will make good any losses I incur, I will make risky $100,000 bets with abandon. This is entirely rational, because if I win, I get to keep the hefty winnings, and if I lose, there is no consequence to me. But note that my incentives—free money from a winning bet—are identical in both situations. What changes my risk-return-ratio and thus my behaviors and choices is the elimination of consequence. And well-intentioned but poorly thought out policies built around rational incentives have a nasty habit of generating unintended consequences, as participants quickly find opportunities to game the system to lower their risk and boost their gain.

So what incentives are presented by the current mode of production? As a general rule, in our current system, moral hazard has been institutionalized; the State is fundamentally a machine for spreading risk to the many while concentrating the gains in the hands of the few. Within the sectors protected or backstopped by the State, moral hazard is heavily incentivized. Why accept the risks of accountability and consequence when they can be offloaded onto others?

Finance is also highly incentivized, because the essence of finance is to obscure risk and offload the costs and consequences to others while reaping the gains upfront. This offloading of risk is the very essence of central and private banking.

Though it is presented as the solution to inequality, State welfare starves its recipients of social and human capital, innovation and initiative—the very assets needed to escape poverty.

Reversing inequality is not incentivized at all in the current mode of production, and so it is unsurprising that alleviating inequality is just a comfortable little pastime for a few privileged do-gooders rather than being the core enterprise of the system.

Neoliberalism, Socialism and Privileged Vested Interests

There are currently two ideologically attractive solutions to inequality and poverty:

- *Neoliberalism*—the opening of new markets and the subsequent exposure of those markets to global competition; and
- *Socialism*, which is, broadly speaking, the public ownership of production along with State-controlled distribution of wages and profits.

Neoliberalism

Neoliberalism has a definitively Jekyll-Hyde nature. While it can increase productivity and competition, and thus help alleviate poverty, it is also a mechanism for consolidating new markets under the control of vested interests.

When neoliberal policies replace vested-interest controlled institutions with opportunities for building capital that are accessible to the majority, these are broadly constructive to the dynamics described by Acemoglu and Robinson in their book *Why Nations Fail* - the democratization of political power and capital-building.

The classic example of liberalization is land reform that breaks up feudal estates into small privately owned farm plots. Freed from the onerous crop-sharing arrangement enforced by the feudal lord, the former serfs become more productive because they get to keep most of their gains in productivity. The liberalization of ownership of the *machinery of value creation* thus fosters broad-based rising prosperity.

This is the basic promise of neoliberalism: by loosening the grip of vested interests and the State, opportunities are opened for the majority who had previously been held down by elites and the State they control.

But this is only the Dr. Jekyll side of neoliberalism. In advanced economies, neoliberal policies may not create broad-based opportunities for all—the policies instead simply substitute new elites for the old ones. A classic example of this is control of a town's water supply.

As an example, neoliberal dogma holds that selling municipally owned water utilities to private owners will lower costs, since competition will be encouraged. Yet the results are precisely the opposite: the local water utility is bought by a global corporation that then raises prices because it is a monopoly—there are no other suppliers of water in town. The citizens are actually worse off in two ways: more of their wealth is extracted by the new private owners, and they have far less influence over the global corporation than they did over the local municipal water utility.

In other words, the democratization of political power and capital-building is not intrinsic to neoliberalism, because opening new markets to competition is only the first step of many. If the ideology of maximizing private gain and the State is left in place, vested interests quickly exploit and take control of the newly opened markets.

Socialism

Socialism suffers from the same fatal flaws as neoliberalism, despite its apparent distance from neoliberalism on the ideological spectrum. Public ownership of the *machinery of value creation* is tailor-made for enforcing the privileges of State-protected vested interests, while it effectively removes all incentives to increase productivity. It also eliminates competition, relegating these disruptive forces to the marginalized informal economy of small businesses such as cafes and farmer's markets.

The only possible solution to inequality is to distribute political power and the opportunities to build capital in a non-politicized (i.e. non-State) decentralized system that cannot be hijacked by vested interests or the State.

Internalizing Privilege and Market/State Pathologies

The vast majority of those who are paid to ponder rising inequality in think-tanks, academia, the State, and non-governmental organizations (NGOs) are well-educated professionals with secure incomes and abundant opportunities to gain recognition and build social capital. Their internalization of the market/State as one of opportunity reflects the fact that they are in the class that is *more equal than others*, i.e. that benefits from the system's inequalities.

It is natural for these comfortable, secure, highly mobile professionals to project their self-satisfaction to everyone else: *the system works great because I'm doing great.* But their experience of the system is limited to their peer group at the top who benefit at the expense of the many.

But below these heights, unrecognized (or even denied) by the elite, the profit-maximizing market/State is experienced as profoundly alienating, anti-social, and inhumane.

The spectrum of human qualities can be viewed as assets much like the limited set of abilities that maximize profit is an asset. The profit-maximizing market exploits all these other assets in service of maximizing profits. Though Marx described the alienation of the worker from the product of his work, the alienation imposed by the profit-maximizing market extends far beyond the broken link between the laborer and the fruits of his/her labor.

The worker's honesty, diligence, trust and sincerity are exploited in service of maximizing profits. In effect, a person's strengths are twisted to serve the employer's profits, requiring habits and behaviors—for example, overworking—that are destructive to the worker and his family.

Human fulfillment in a profit-maximizing market is *derealized* into a private enterprise, where the isolated individual no longer regards the social order as a potential cause of his alienation - but instead looks to religion, psychotherapy or medications as private solutions to the sociopathology he inhabits. Even if an individual does recognize that the social order is the cause of his distress, he is channeled into self-medicating by the awareness that he is powerless to change the system.

In this carefully cultivated sphere of profit-maximizing individuality, it is absolute heresy to suggest that human fulfillment has a communal, social quality—that fulfillment is essentially impossible in a system that reduces all human qualities to profit and control.

The essence of State welfare is that all the layers of human community—reciprocity, obligation, duty, the joy of sharing and of sacrifice—are marginalized by the State, because the individual receives cash directly from the State not because of their actions or their efforts on behalf of others -but simply because they are drawing breath.

And it is necessary for the State to do this in order to reduce the individual and the community as threats to State power.

In the impersonal system of State-issued welfare, there is no need to recognize the needs of others, to share the tasks that benefit all or make any sacrifices in the spirit of reciprocity; instead the State meets all the needs of the individual without demanding anything in exchange except dependence on the State.

Thus State welfare is not only anti-social; it is profoundly inhumane. It strips away the community that gives individuals meaning and purpose. In the State welfare system, the individual is reduced to a consumer of corporate goods and services and paid by the State, an isolated, self-absorbed individual stripped of communal identity and personal agency.

Just as the market seeks to make every human interaction into a profitable financial transaction, the State seeks to control each participant by making them financially dependent on the State. Once the individual has been reduced to dependence on the State, they are passive, complicit and compliant - because any resistance to the State raises the threat of being cut off from the State's largesse. This is how social welfare starves its recipients of social and human capital, innovation and initiative—the very assets needed to assemble wealth-creating capital and escape poverty.

This systemic reduction of human qualities and community to serve the needs of the profit-maximizing market and the State is *derealized* into a false worship of profit, State power and the individual's quest for solace in a world that strips away the very qualities needed for fulfillment, meaning, purpose and community.

Humans draw their purpose and self-worth from *producing*, not *consuming*, and from belonging to a group that provides a larger goal than self-indulgence, which is the ultimate objective of consumerism. The profit-maximizing market and the State strip away these two essentials by turning producers into consumers and groups into atomized, isolated individuals dependent on the State.

I discuss this subtle process of derealization further in my book *Resistance, Revolution, Liberation.*

It is ironic that the well-paid professionals in the charity/welfare industry have internalized the derealized fantasy of the market/State system so completely that they are blind to their own profound alienation. Instead, they project their failure onto those trapped in a system that is, in reality, structured so the *only possible output is exploitation, alienation, the destruction of community, and the rise of anti-social pathologies.*

Defending Charity and Welfare Assuages Guilt and Validates Privilege

If we are truly honest, we must face the disturbing truth that defending charity and State welfare is not about fixing inequality as much as assuaging our guilt that we're benefiting from a system that is rigged in favor of the few at the expense of the many. Defending programs that not just fail to end poverty but actively strip the recipients of agency and make them dependent on our aid serves two purposes: it solidifies the dominance of the system that benefits us, and it gives us the high moral ground where we can self-righteously celebrate our moral superiority as generous donors.

Why do we continue to defend programs that produce so little sustainable results? Why do we tolerate the corruption, waste and poor results from such gargantuan investments? Because the results matter less than reducing our guilt through the act of giving, which magically transforms our guilt into self-righteousness.

Our outrage at such accusations is a measure of the truth of the accusation.

Why are our expectations of the charity/welfare industry so much lower than our expectations of profit-seeking enterprise? Why do we tolerate levels of failure that would be unacceptable in enterprise?

One reason is the guilt, but another is because *actually reversing inequality would threaten the system that currently benefits us*. Not only does the current world-system reward us as being *more equal than others*, it validates our moral superiority as selfless donors and supporters of charity/welfare.

Another reason is that solving poverty would up-end the *raison d'etre* of the plummy anti-poverty programs of the foundations, NGOs and State agencies. Who wants to solve a problem that their industry needs to sustain its own survival?

Perpetuating poverty validates the privileges of the few; we few at the top of the moral and financial pyramid can *express our moral superiority while supporting programs that are designed to fail*. The failure of charity/welfare ensures we can continue to occupy the high moral ground and act out our role as saviors to the benighted poor.

If we are truly sincere about reversing inequality, we must come to grips with the reality that the *charity/welfare industry perpetuates inequality by design*.

The solution to rising inequality is not a system that provides privilege-validating charity. The solution to rising inequality is a system that reduces inequality as *the only possible output of the system*.

Chapter Seven - The Nature of Social Privilege

Social Privilege and Social Capital

Just as the State does not outlaw competition that threatens privileged classes but instead simply makes competition impossibly costly and complex, social privilege relies not on legal barriers but on informal barriers that *limit access to positions of privilege and social capital*. These are the barriers of *invitation* and *private access* - invisible and unspoken, but real nonetheless.

For example, since one way to gain privilege is to marry into a wealthy, powerful family, the pool of potential mates must be limited to those of the same class. Members of the unprotected, unprivileged class are not invited to poolside parties, except perhaps as a recruiting tool, but even if they are granted access, it's made crystal clear that the owner's sons and daughters are off-limits.

Since friendships made in school tend to influence career choices, marriage prospects, etc., the privileged class enrolls its children in private prep schools and elite universities, both to prepare them for service in their class and to ensure their friends will belong to their class or be talented and ambitious enough to navigate the many barriers.

The barriers often involve exclusions: female managers are not invited on hunting/fishing trips with top management, with the excuses being they wouldn't feel comfortable, their childcare responsibilities, etc. The unprivileged are not invited to join golf games, exclusive clubs, boards of directors of charitable organizations, fundraisers, and other clubby communities of privilege.

The especially talented outsider might be invited in to perform some onerous task or to help with the organization's functions (perhaps to demonstrate that the organization is 'open', 'unbiased' and 'politically correct'), but they won't be invited out after the meeting for drinks—and if they are, the awkward silences and insiders' jokes will make it clear that they don't belong and never will.

What is being husbanded and protected is *social capital*: personal relationships, networks of influential people, and access to movers and shakers and people in positions of power.

Unlike financial capital, social capital is difficult to measure but instantly recognizable: it is intangible, and its power rests on trust, accountability, reciprocity and discretion. Yet despite its ephemeral nature, social capital is the key that opens access to the other forms of capital: intellectual, cultural and financial. The unprivileged may slip through the barriers with a bit of luck, but having a mentor on the inside who uses his/her social capital to open doors is much better than mere luck.

Social capital has its own set of strict rules, the most important of which is that personal relationships are not to be exploited exclusively for private gain. Rather, social capital is based on reciprocity and the protection of privileged positions and networks.

If for example I recommend a young woman to a senior director based on her merit and values (i.e. she is trustworthy, polite, hardworking, accountable, exhibits self-control and won't overstep her position), and the young protégé immediately exploits her position in the senior director's circle, this would damage the social capital of everyone involved.

Clearly, the young woman wasn't qualified in terms of cultural and social capital to function in the privileged position, and my own social capital would be damaged by my recommendation. I would have to rebuild my social capital, perhaps by adding the senior director's recommended protégé to my staff and ensuring she has ample opportunities to build social capital within my network.

Recall from Chapter One that privilege is largely a matter of position rather than merit, although merit may have been a factor in the individual's ascent. As noted earlier, the gains from privilege are asymmetrical, meaning that the opportunities to build capital in a position of privilege are far more expansive than the opportunities available at the merely advantaged levels. To use stock options as a financial example: the employee in an advantaged position might earn 10,000 options after years of productive service, while the person in a privileged position gets 100,000 options just for occupying the position.

The opportunities for building social capital are equally asymmetric. Befriending people in positions of power greatly expands one's own opportunities to build financial, intellectual and social capital.

Compare the social capital of an unprivileged person in a disadvantaged neighborhood with that of a person who attended prep school and university and whose parents introduced them to a social circle rich in social capital.

Which individual is more likely to have opportunities to build capital in all its forms?

Social capital does not lend itself to legal enforcement. It isn't possible, nor is it ethical, to enforce who gets to marry whom, or who gets to meet or befriend whom.

The solution to inequality is not to attempt to restrict the social capital of the privileged, but to create an infrastructure in which anyone with the requisite ambition and personal values can build social capital, and do so without any gate keeper's permission.

In my book *Get a Job, Build a Real Career and Defy a Bewildering Economy*, I describe the *eight essential skills* needed to build capital in all its forms. These skills are accessible to anyone, as they are values-based rather than skill-based. A person doesn't need to earn a high SAT score to acquire the eight essential skills; all they need is the will to do so.

In the current social order, the way to build social capital is to join a privileged class. The problem is that the doors to the privileged class are narrow and heavily guarded by gate keepers. Few will gain access, and so privilege is maintained, not eroded.

On the other hand, technology offers the potential to create an *infrastructure of opportunity* that *is* open to all. I describe an educational infrastructure of opportunity in my book *The Nearly Free University*, and a larger global infrastructure of opportunity in *A Radically Beneficial World*.

The only way to reverse rising inequality is to open opportunities to build capital in all its forms to everyone. Rather than make the process a matter of luck or squeezing through narrow doors to a privileged class, we need structures that enable anyone to advance from the disadvantaged class to the advantaged class and join networks that build social capital.

Social privilege is the power to limit access to social capital. The solution is to open access to social capital to everyone who is willing to invest their trust, accountability, reciprocity and discretion.

Chapter Eight - The End Game: Crisis and the Collapse of Privilege

Profound systemic changes do not occur in stable eras, for the simple reason that there is no overriding need to accept the risks of making new arrangements if all is well (or at least tolerable). Transformation only becomes possible when the current arrangement is visibly failing. It usually takes a systemic crisis to open the door to structural change; otherwise those benefiting from the current mode of production will fight to maintain their privileges with every resource available.

Prior to complete systemic failure, incremental modifications may be allowed—what I call *policy tweaks*—as long as they leave the current distribution of wealth and power unchanged. But small policy tweaks cannot stop or reverse the decay of an unsustainable system.

Systems that protect privilege cripple the very dynamics of sustainable self-regulation and widespread prosperity: competition, innovation, dissent and social mobility. Privilege acts as a tax not just on the unprivileged but on the economy as a whole. The dead hand of privilege doesn't just siphon off wealth; it institutionalizes perverse incentives and robs the system of vitality by diverting capital from productive investment to the pockets of the privileged.

If privilege was merely a matter of overcompensating a tiny handful of neofeudal nobility, the system could bear this rentier burden. But privilege is now built into the primary structure of our entire mode of production: the way we create and distribute money and credit at the top of the wealth/power pyramid, the pay-to-play racketeering of centralized political power, and the offloading of risk (i.e. *skin in the game*) from the protected privileged classes to the unprotected unprivileged.

Risk can never be extinguished; it can only be transferred. The privileged classes believe they have magically eliminated their own risk by offloading it onto the unprivileged. But in reality all they've really done is transfer the risks of financial and moral bankruptcy onto the system itself. As a result, the system itself is made increasingly fragile and unstable.

Defending privilege generates self-reinforcing and self-defeating feedback loop. By repressing dissent, competition, innovation and social mobility, the privileged are fatally weakening the system that feeds them. In protecting privilege, the status quo is destroying the only possible solution to the problem.

Policy tweaks create the comforting illusion of reform, but the collapse of privilege and the entire mode of production is the only possible outcome of the system as it is currently structured.

This leads to a profound conclusion: the only way to avoid collapse is to change the mode of production at its very foundation--how money and capital are created and distributed—for these are the sources of inequality and stagnation. The only possible outcome of inequality is stagnation, fragility, instability and collapse.

In the current arrangement, money is borrowed into existence at rates that favor the privileged and punish the unprivileged. The privileged borrow money to buy income-producing assets, while the unprivileged borrow money just to survive. The only possible outcome of this system is the rich get richer and the poor get poorer.

In a knowledge/finance based economy, access to intangible capital (human, intellectual, cultural and social capital) and to money at its source are the keys to reversing inequality and alleviating poverty, which are first and foremost the consequence of a lack of capital in all its forms. But since reforming the structures defended by self-serving elites that own the machinery of governance is impossible, *the only solution is to create infrastructures of opportunity that are independent of the current system of money, credit, capital and pay-to-play politics.*

Here are the key requirements of an alternative system that can self-organize in the shadows of the status quo without directly challenging it:

- A decentralized form of money that is distributed to those at the bottom of the wealth/power pyramid who are producing goods and services to meet the needs of their community.
- This money cannot be borrowed into existence; it must be issued in exchange for productive work done on behalf of the community, and free of any payment of interest.
- An open-source software platform that creates a clear path from the disadvantaged class to the advantaged class, a path that enables everyone, regardless of class, to assemble capital in all its forms.
- An open-source software platform that strips out bias and privilege by treating every individual equally.

I have described this type of decentralized, opt-in, self-organizing system that makes money and capital accessible to every participant in my book *A Radically Beneficial World: Automation, Technology and Creating Jobs for All.*

We don't have a choice about the current arrangement collapsing; there is no other possible outcome other than collapse. However, we do have a choice about what system will arise to replace it. If it is based on protecting privilege, it too will collapse, for the same reasons the current arrangement is collapsing.

Technology has opened up new ways of organizing our mode of production and our social/political orders. A decentralized, opt-in, largely automated infrastructure of opportunity would be fairer, more efficient, more sustainable, and systemically moral—everything the current status quo is not.

How can we start to make such a system real? The first step is simply to imagine it...

* * *

By design, this book is a brief overview of a complex web of interconnected topics. I have addressed many of these topics in greater depth in my previous books: *Resistance, Revolution, Liberation; The Nearly Free University; Get a Job, Build a Real Career* and *A Radically Beneficial World.* I invite you to explore these ideas further in these more comprehensive books.

Charles Hugh Smith

Berkeley, California USA

October 2016

Made in the USA
Monee, IL
12 January 2021